An *Assembly* for **Europe**

The Council of Europe's Parliamentary Assembly 1949-1989

Bruno Haller

Council of Europe Publishing

French edition: *Une Assemblée au service de l'Europe*

ISBN-10: 92-871-5924-6
ISBN-13: 978-92-871-5924-3

The opinions expressed in this work are the responsibility of the author(s) and do not necessarily reflect the official policy of the Council of Europe.

All rights reserved. No part of this publication may be translated, reproduced or transmitted, in any form or by any means, electronic (CD-Rom, Internet, etc.) or mechanical, including photocopying, recording or any information storage or retrieval system, without prior permission in writing from the Public Information and Publications Division, Directorate of Communication (F-67075 Strasbourg Cedex or publishing@coe.int).

As far as possible we have mentioned the names of the rights holders of the photographs and illustrations in this publication. We apologise for any errors or omissions and will ensure that these are corrected in future editions.

Photographs: © Council of Europe
Cover and layout design: Graphic Design Workshop, Council of Europe
Page layout: DTP Unit, Council of Europe

Council of Europe Publishing
F-67075 Strasbourg Cedex
http://book.coe.int

ISBN-10: 92-871-6029-5
ISBN-13: 978-92-871-6029-4

© Council of Europe, December 2006
Printed in France by Valblor

Contents

Foreword	5
Preface	7
Chapter 1: *Foundation and first members*	15
Chapter 2: *Shaping the new Europe*	43
Chapter 3: *Making laws for Europe*	65
Chapter 4: *No to capital punishment*	87
Chapter 5: *The Mediterranean dimension*	103
Chapter 6: *The Assembly – source of ideas, beacon of democracy*	139
Chapter 7: *Expanding in the West, opening to the East*	175
List of Presidents and Clerks/Secretaries General of the Assembly	222
List of Secretaries General and Deputy Secretaries General of the Council of Europe	223
The Assembly in brief	225

Foreword

■ **René van der Linden**
President of the Parliamentary Assembly

Founded over 50 years ago, to ensure that future generations would never again know horrors like those of the Second World War, the Council of Europe is a unique intergovernmental organisation, with a parliamentary body which has, in the last 50 years, become its heart – and the heart of greater Europe with its 800 million people.

In this book, Bruno Haller takes us on a fascinating tour through the story of the Council of Europe's Parliamentary Assembly, paying it a deeply felt tribute in the process. With exemplary care and scrupulous attention to detail, he traces changes in its role from 1949 to 1989, and shows how it helped the Council of Europe to expand and develop.

Thanks to his 10 years as the Assembly's Secretary General, the picture he paints of some of the turning points in Europe's recent past is unusually vivid. Drawing on his vast experience and, above all, deep-seated commitment to building a Europe united by shared values, he shows us – experts and general readers alike – just how much this unique democratic institution has to offer. All the more reason to look forward to his promised second volume.

Building Europe is a rational process, which is why ideas and ideals are important. But heart and commitment are needed as well, to make sure that the human dimension comes first. At a time when Euroscepticism seems the dominant mood, I am convinced that Bruno Haller's book will help to rekindle belief in a strong Europe – and a Europe in which human rights really count.

Preface

■ **Bruno Haller**
Secretary General of the Parliamentary Assembly

For 10 years, my office at the Council of Europe has given me a breathtaking view of Strasbourg Cathedral which, with its single spire, always makes me think of a hand pointing skyward from the city clustered at its base.

Because the work took longer than expected, because there were problems with the site and subsoil, and because the money quite simply ran out, the planned second spire was never added – but the cathedral remains a masterpiece of Gothic architecture, one of Europe's greatest treasures and a major source of pride to Alsatians like myself. It has come to symbolise Strasbourg, and its single spire makes it utterly distinctive, giving it a unique silhouette which Europeans (and not just Europeans) instantly recognise.

Strasbourg is the Council of Europe's home city, and in some ways the stories of the Council's Parliamentary Assembly and Strasbourg's cathedral are not entirely dissimilar. Like the cathedral, the Assembly – the first European forum of elected national members of parliament (MPs) – was a visionary, groundbreaking project.

Again like the cathedral, it had a difficult birth. The founding governments wanted an organisation which would promote democracy and protect human rights, but some of them thought that an intergovernmental body, with no parliamentary supervision, would suffice for that purpose.

Like the cathedral, the Assembly which eventually emerged from the diplomatic wrangling was short of one planned element: it had consultative status – but no decision-making powers.

And yet, like the builders of the cathedral, who defied all obstacles to produce a miracle in stone, the members of the Assembly stood firm, got their way and ultimately made it a respected and influential partner in building the new Europe.

When it was founded, the Council of Europe was Europe's only political organisation, and the challenge it faced was enormous: reconciling and reconstructing a Europe devastated by the war, and deeply traumatised by the Nazis' total negation of human dignity in the death camps. The breadth of the Assembly's vision was displayed at its very first session in August 1949, when it called for Germany's admission, and laid the foundations of a new European order by recommending preparation of three historic treaties: the European Convention on Human Rights, the European Social Charter and the European Cultural Convention.

A Europe for Europeans, made by Europeans – this, from the start, was the founding fathers' goal in planning Europe's future. Success, they realised, would depend on identifying, and meeting, Europeans' aspirations. The Assembly itself immediately saw that transparency, accountability and democracy were essential features of the European project, and that its members, elected by their fellow citizens to speak for them, must be able to make themselves heard – and share in decision-making.

The Council of Europe's story can be divided into two main periods: before and after the fall of the Berlin Wall in 1989.

The first period – the subject of this volume – saw the Organisation's membership grow by easy stages from 10 to 23, taking in nearly all the west European democracies by the time Finland joined on 5 May 1989.

The archives from that period are a treasure-house for researchers, but still remain largely untapped.

In the first 10 years of its existence, the Assembly was forum and forge – the place where the new Europe was talked into being and hammered into shape. Nearly all the great Europeans, statesmen like Winston Churchill, Alcide de Gasperi, Konrad Adenauer and Robert Schuman, came to its rostrum to expound their visions of the continent's future, proclaim their hopes, and sometimes – like Paul-Henri Spaak – acknowledge their disappointments. All the European projects, and particularly those aimed at establishing smaller, tighter communities, were discussed in it. Whatever the issue, however, there was always a burning determination to preserve the Council of Europe's role as the European project's political core.

The Assembly's second decade was a time when European integration was making good headway in Brussels and Luxembourg. The Assembly backed the process, and suggested formal ties between the European Community and the Council of Europe, which it saw – and still sees – as the main institutional architects of European unity.

It was also determined, however, that the Council of Europe must use its own powers to the full, and played an active part in framing its new work programme. This was geared to intergovernmental co-operation in eight different fields, and gave the Organisation an eminently practical part in shaping the new Europe.

The Assembly itself made suggestions and launched initiatives in all the work programme areas – particularly legal co-operation, where it took the lead by proposing new conventions and agreements.

The first period also saw reverses – military takeovers in Greece and later Turkey. The Assembly reacted as a political body, and also as the ever-watchful guardian of the Council's principles. Essentially, its approach was based on keeping the door open – as it did with Portugal and Spain at a very early stage by contacting their democratic oppositions, and so smoothing the way to Council membership for both.

It also played a driving role in campaigning for abolition of the death penalty in the member states – a campaign now regarded as emblematic of the Council of Europe's work for human rights in general.

True, a Europe-wide ban on capital punishment did not come into being until the Council had admitted the former Communist countries, but the first political moves towards that final, spectacular breakthrough had been made long before; indeed the Assembly first called on the member states to halt executions in the early 1970s.

Also significant was the Assembly's decision to drop its original qualifier, "consultative", and style itself "parliamentary" Assembly. The new title, which was truer to its character and the role it intended to play at the Council of Europe, was approved by the Committee of Ministers in February 1994.

People sometimes think that the Council of Europe's interest in the countries of central and eastern Europe is recent, and was prompted by the massive political upheavals which accompanied the fall of the Berlin Wall. But the

Assembly had never forgotten the dream of its founders, and its interest in the East – reflected in its championing of the "captive nations" in the 1950s, its desire to make the Council of Europe a platform for East-West negotiation in the late 1960s, and its attempt to become the Assembly of the Organization for Security and Co-operation in Europe (OSCE) in the early 1990s – has been constant from the start.

For the Council of Europe as a whole, 1989 was a watershed year. The Assembly introduced "special guest status" for east European parliaments which wanted closer ties with Strasbourg. In July 1989, it welcomed Mikhail Gorbachev, whose vision of a "common European home" seemed to echo certain aspects of Winston Churchill's famous speech of 1946. From that point on, the momentum increased, as the former Soviet countries threw off the totalitarian yoke and made a determined bid for freedom, at last healing the ideological rift which had divided Europe for the previous half-century.

A new era dawned, a profoundly different Europe emerged – and the Council of Europe remade itself as a pan-European body. Once more, as my second volume will show, the Assembly played a leading part in the process.

Locals and visitors in Strasbourg often complain that, because of restoration work on the cathedral, its soaring beauty is almost always masked by scaffolding. None of this present activity means that the medieval masons got things wrong or used poor materials – just that working on a grandiose structure of this kind is, by definition, a never-ending process. And the same is true of working on democracy and human rights.

My hope is that this book will take readers into the heart of that other great project which is under way in Strasbourg, with the Assembly as one of its chief architects – the building of a united Europe.

The hundreds of documents and speeches I have had to read while writing it have made the Assembly seem a living presence and have given me a sense of sharing directly in its hopes, disappointments and doubts – and also its constantly renewed faith in the European project. I have not, alas, been able to cover all aspects of its work in the 40 years I am describing – which is why I have chosen, in this book, to focus on its political activity. I now leave my readers to discover the dynamic role it has played in shaping Europe's recent past and helping to bring the European vision to fruition. I invite them to join me in reliving this epic journey which I – thanks to my years at the Council of Europe – have had the privilege of following from the inside.

Acknowledgements

My thanks to journalist Michel Arnould for his help with several parts of this book, and to Alexandra Alléon for her unfailing support while I was writing it.

Without Mario Heinrich and his encyclopaedic knowledge of the Council of Europe and its past, and without Kathleen Layle, I could never have completed my research. My warmest thanks to both, and to Francesc Ferrer for his many valuable and creative suggestions.

My thanks, too, to Simon Newman for his help during the final stages of the project.

Bruno Haller

1

Foundation and first members

"We desire a united Europe, throughout whose area the free movement of persons, ideas and goods is restored. […] We desire a European Assembly where the live forces of all our nations shall be represented."

■ **"Message to Europeans",** adopted at the final session of the European Congress, The Hague, 7-10 May 1948.

Foundation and first members

"I trust that the European family can act unitedly as one under a Council of Europe."
Winston Churchill, October 1942.

THE ZURICH SPARK

The Council of Europe's founding fathers are too numerous to be listed fully here. The best known is Winston Churchill, who first proposed a Council of Europe in the darkest days of the Second World War. At a time when the outcome was anything but certain, he firmly believed the democracies would triumph, and already looked ahead to a time when the free world would reorganise under the auspices of a global organisation, the future United Nations, and regional organisations, such as a Council of Europe and a Council of Asia. *"I trust that the European family can act unitedly as one under a Council of Europe. I look forward to a United States of Europe in which barriers between the nations will be greatly minimised and unrestricted travel will be possible"*, he declared in a letter to the War Cabinet in October 1942.

THE UNITED STATES OF EUROPE

Speaking in Zurich shortly after the war, on 19 September 1946, Churchill – statesman, war-time leader, but no longer head of government – painted a commanding picture of his ideal united Europe. The occasion was not formal, the speech was not official, and his audience were not politicians or diplomats, but students – Europe's young people and its future. In the circumstances of the time, his message – he called on the European family to reunite on the basis of Franco-German partnership – was nothing short of sensational. *"Our constant aim must be to*

Foundation and first members

■ **Winston Churchill,**
Place Kléber, Strasbourg,
12 August 1949.

"We are reunited here, in this new Assembly, not as representatives of our several countries or various political parties, but as Europeans forging ahead, hand in hand, and if necessary elbow to elbow, to restore the former glories of Europe and to permit this illustrious continent to take its place once more, in a world organisation, as an independent member sufficient unto itself. That primary and sacred loyalty that one owes to one's own country is not difficult to reconcile with this larger feeling of European fellowship."

build and fortify the strength of the United Nations Organisation. Under and within that world concept we must recreate the European family in a regional structure called, it may be, the United States of Europe. And the first practical step would be to form a Council of Europe. If at first all the states of Europe are not willing or able to join the union, we must nevertheless proceed to assemble and combine those who will and those who can.

The salvation of the common people of every race and of every land from war or servitude must be established on solid foundations and must be guarded by the readiness of all men and women to die rather than submit to tyranny. In all this urgent work, France and Germany must take the lead together. Great Britain, the British Commonwealth of Nations, mighty America and I trust Soviet Russia – for then indeed all would be well – must be the friends and sponsors of the new Europe and must champion its right to live and shine. Therefore I say to you: Let Europe arise!"

FIRST NECESSITY: RECONCILE FRANCE AND GERMANY

Churchill proclaimed two crystal-clear objectives: Europe must be reunited, and France and Germany reconciled. It was still too soon to do the second, as the peoples on either side of the Rhine were still nursing their wounds. Nonetheless, Churchill had stated the principle that any policy aimed at building Europe must take reconciliation as its basis. Indeed, all the

European initiatives which came afterwards showed that he had not simply outlined his vision of the future Europe, but had actually laid its foundations.

Public enthusiasm for Europe had long been nurtured by projects put forward by intellectuals, philosophers and politicians – men like the Austrian diplomat, Richard Coudenhove-Kalergi, the Spanish writer, Salvador de Madariaga, and the French politicians, Aristide Briand and Edouard Herriot. But it was the traumatic experience of the war which led the various groups to unite and found the "European Movement" in 1947.

EUROPE MUST UNITE!

When they met in London in December 1947, the foreign ministers of the wartime allies (the United States, France, the United Kingdom and the Soviet Union) were unable to agree on the German question and on a new European order. Speaking in the House of Commons shortly afterwards, on 22 January 1948, British Foreign Secretary, Ernest Bevin, declared that the time had come to unite western Europe, and suggested that France, the United Kingdom, Belgium, the Netherlands and Luxembourg form an association based on fundamental freedoms and shared ethical values. This proposal led to the Brussels Treaty of 17 March 1948, forerunner of the Western European Union (WEU) Treaty, and to the European Congress in The Hague.

Traumatic memories of the war were the unifying force behind the "European Movement", founded in 1947.

Foundation and first members

THE HAGUE CONGRESS, 1948

A federal Europe or a Europe based on intergovernmental co-operation? The congress was divided.

Public feeling and the thinking of Europe's leading politicians and intellectuals fused as never before at The Hague Congress, which met in 1948 to plan the continent's future. Chaired by Winston Churchill, the congress was attended by some 750 delegates from 17 countries – the 10 which went on to found the Council of Europe, plus Germany, Austria, Greece, Iceland, Liechtenstein, Switzerland and Turkey. The participants included statesmen, parliamentarians, philosophers, trade unionists, journalists, bankers, industrialists and religious leaders, genuinely speaking for all sections of European society. Observer delegations came from Finland, Spain, six central and east European countries (Bulgaria, Hungary, Poland, Romania, Czechoslovakia and Yugoslavia), the United States and Canada. When it came to deciding whether the aim should be a federal Europe, or a Europe based on intergovernmental co-operation, the congress was divided. Nonetheless, it came up with three important proposals: economic and political union to guarantee security and social progress; a European assembly; and a human rights charter, with a European court of justice to enforce it.

The European assembly envisaged by The Hague Congress was later embodied in the Council of Europe's Assembly.

AN ASSEMBLY – WHAT KIND? AN ORGANISATION – WHAT NAME?

Immediately after The Hague Congress, in autumn 1948, the Committee for the Study of European Unity, chaired by Edouard Herriot, President of the French National Assembly, started drafting the Council of Europe's founding treaty, which was finalised at ambassadorial and ministerial conferences held in London in spring 1949. Some serious differences had needed settling first. France and Belgium, who saw the new organisation as the first step towards European union, had wanted to give it a genuine parliamentary assembly, with wide-ranging powers and elected members independent of governments. Britain, on the other hand, wanted an old-style organisation, geared to intergovernmental co-operation, directed by a committee of ministers, and backed by a consultative assembly which had no decision-making powers and was not genuinely parliamentary.

A compromise was finally agreed in January 1949 by the French and British foreign ministers, Robert Schuman and Ernest Bevin. The resultant Council of Europe had a Committee of Ministers (a decision-making body comprising the member states' foreign ministers) and a Consultative Assembly (a deliberative body comprising members of national parliaments).

The ambassadorial conference had left the final decision on the organisation's name to the ministerial conference, which met on 4 and 5 May 1949. Here again, opinions were divided. Some of the ministers, like Robert Schuman, favoured "European

Foundation and first members

■ **The Committee of Ministers' first session,**
Strasbourg Town Hall,
8 August 1949.

Union", which underlined the ambitious nature of the project. Many felt, however, that this suggested a federation of states – and so "Council of Europe" carried the day.

EUROPE'S FIRST POLITICAL INSTITUTION

The Council of Europe was officially born in London on 5 May 1949. Strasbourg, a city scarred by three Franco-German wars in less than a century, and so a fitting focus for hopes of reconciliation between the two countries, was its chosen location. The Treaty of London was signed by ten states: Belgium, Denmark, France, Ireland, Italy, Luxembourg, the Netherlands, Norway, Sweden and the United Kingdom.

The Council was given a wide-ranging brief, national defence being the only omission from the list. Great hopes were pinned on it, as the first – and, until the Treaty of Rome brought the European Economic Community into being in 1957, only – general political organisation dealing with nearly all the issues which mattered in Europe.

FIRST MEETING OF THE COMMITTEE OF MINISTERS…

On 8 August 1949, French Foreign Minister Robert Schuman opened the first meeting of the brand-new organisation's Committee of Ministers at Strasbourg Town Hall. One of its first decisions was to invite Greece and Turkey to join the ten founder

Many people felt that "European Union" suggested a federation – and so "Council of Europe" was chosen.

members, which they did the following day. The same invitation went to Iceland, which joined on 7 March 1950.

... AND THE ASSEMBLY

On 10 August 1949, the Assembly of the Council of Europe held its first session in the main lecture theatre at Strasbourg University.

On 10 August 1949, the Council of Europe's Assembly met for the first time in the main lecture theatre at Strasbourg University. Opening the session, Edouard Herriot, the Honorary President, declared: *"Your Statute has instructed you to give form to the aspirations of the peoples of Europe and to furnish the governments with the means of keeping constantly in touch with European public opinion. There is no question of organising or preparing a military alliance; it is simply a question of safeguarding and realising the ideals which are the common heritage of the participating members. We are not declaring war on anyone. Whatever may be alleged, our meetings have no aggressive intentions towards anybody. We merely desire to associate ourselves in order to defend those two great acquisitions of human civilisation: freedom and law."*

The following day, the Assembly elected Paul-Henri Spaak (Belgium) as its President. In a brief inaugural speech, he summarised the aims and aspirations of the Council of Europe and the Assembly, declaring that justice, law and liberty, which must be the new Europe's ideals, had triumphed. He went on: *"Now, one might always say suddenly, the glorious dream we dreamed when we were young, the dream we thought unattainable and*

Foundation and first members

■ **Edouard Herriot, Honorary President,**
*at the Assembly's inaugural session, Strasbourg University,
10 August 1949.*

"Your Statute has instructed you to give form to the aspirations of the peoples of Europe and to furnish the governments with the means of keeping constantly in touch with European public opinion. There is no question of organising or preparing a military alliance; it is simply a question of safeguarding and realising the ideals which are the common heritage of the participating members."

sometimes despaired of realising, is taking shape – and we are trying here in Strasbourg to make it a living reality." From the very first day, he also insisted that strengthening the Assembly held one of the keys to the Council of Europe's future. *"This Assembly is now gathered together. It is undoubtedly the most important body within the Council of Europe. […] It is my wish, and I am sure it is yours too, that it should be strong, independent and practical."*

In fact, the Assembly immediately complained of its "subordinate status" under the treaty, demanding greater powers and a bigger role within the Council of Europe. Specifically, it felt that the Committee of Ministers should allow it to decide its own agenda, and consult it on admitting new members.

On 10 August, the Assembly also welcomed the representatives of Greece and Turkey, which had been admitted to the Council of Europe the day before. Speaking on 16 August, Greek MP Leon Maccas declared: *"With us, Europe can and must become a continuous creation, a living, moving, coherent and flexible organism. How shall we achieve this? By European federalism or by mere co-operation among European countries? […] Today, we can no longer think, act, live or hope anything from the future if we do not break down our national barriers, and shake up our national organisations. The reason is that life today only recognises much larger units – in the future this will increasingly be the case – formed under the influence of a common conception of life and a common civilisation. […] Finally, as European civilisation is a unity, so Europe must also be a unity, and we ourselves must be the expression of that united Europe."* His Turkish fellow-member, Kasim Gulek, made a similar point when he insisted: *"What we are working for here is not only union of one part of Europe, but union of the whole of Europe. It is true that parts of Europe are represented here today, but it is our great hope that some day all the countries and peoples of Europe will be represented in this Assembly, which will be a real parliament of Europe. In the union we are after, linguistic, religious and other distinctions count for nothing. Human freedom and willingness to work together are the criteria that count for us. Our door is open to all European nations which are, or will be, ready to work with us in this direction."*

THE COUNCIL OF EUROPE'S FIRST SECRETARY GENERAL

As first Secretary General of the Council of Europe, the Assembly chose Jacques Camille Paris, a French diplomat and former executive secretary of the Preparatory Committee on the Council of Europe, which had been set up by the ministerial conference in London and continued to function until August 1949. To underline its administrative autonomy within the Council of Europe, it claimed the right to elect its own Chief of Administrative Services, and duly chose Prince Caracciolo di Castagneto to fill this post a year later.

■ **Jacques Camille Paris,**
the Council of Europe's first Secretary General,
August 1949.

Foundation and first members

GERMANY JOINS

German membership was already an issue at the Assembly's first session. Speaking on 17 August, Winston Churchill declared: *"I now come to the greatest and most important of all the questions that are before us. A united Europe cannot live without the help and strength of Germany. […] One of the most practical reasons for pressing forward with the creation of a European assembly was that it provided an effective means, and possibly the only immediately effective means, of associating a democratic and free Germany with the western democracies."*

■ **Winston Churchill,**
speaking before the Assembly,
17 August 1949.

In fact, as soon as it had been refounded on a democratic basis, with Konrad Adenauer as its first Chancellor, the Federal Republic of Germany was invited to join the Council of Europe. It became an associate member on 13 July 1950, and delegates from Germany, and also Iceland and the Saar, attended the Assembly's August session. In his welcoming speech, President Spaak declared: *"The entry into this Assembly of the delegates of Germany, Iceland and the Saar is manifestly an event of great historical importance for us. As we all know, the Europe of which we talk is, alas! a mutilated Europe. In view of the gravity of the problems that we now have to face, we must gather together all of our remaining forces to work for the common good. I feel that our new colleagues will bring with them to this Assembly their high capacities and their goodwill. With their aid we can make this second session a success of such an order that, when we disperse, public opinion will be more convinced than ever before of the indestructible and eternal mission of Europe."*

Replying, Hermann Pünder of the German delegation said: *"Mr President, on behalf of my German fellow countrymen, I thank you for your cordial words of welcome. I would also like to thank my eminent colleagues for the kind applause with which they greeted your words. We, the German representatives in this Assembly, belong to different political parties, and our political opinions are not all the same. We have not been nominated by a government. We have been elected by the Parliament of the German Federal Republic. In the letter of invitation sent to our government by the Committee of Ministers, it was stated that, when the German Federal Republic was invited to join the Assembly, this meant that Germany would become an integral part of the European states assembled here. We who are here are thus the representatives of Germany as a whole. The German representatives, representing as they do an associate member and a country which has not yet been granted a peace treaty, are now here to co-operate with you in all consciousness and good faith in establishing a politically, economically and constitutionally united Europe, forming one people free and equal before the law."*

Germany went on to become a full member on 2 May 1951.

"The entry into this Assembly of the delegates of Germany, Iceland and the Saar is manifestly an event of great historical importance for us. As we all know, the Europe of which we talk is, alas! a mutilated Europe."
Paul-Henri Spaak, 13 July 1950.

Foundation and first members

AUSTRIA FOLLOWS

Austria did not join until 1956, but its links with the Council were far older. At the very beginning, in May 1948, it had sent a 12-member delegation to The Hague Congress. One of those members was Eduard Ludwig, who attended the Assembly's inaugural session in Strasbourg in August 1949, and went on to become Austria's observer at the Council in 1953.

In 1949, the Assembly asked the Committee of Ministers to consider admitting new members and associates; Germany, Austria and the Saarland were its candidates.

In Recommendation 7 of 6 September 1949, the Assembly – thinking of Germany, Austria and the Saarland – asked the Committee of Ministers to examine the possibility of admitting new members and associates. The Committee favoured doing this as soon as possible, but felt that a final decision on Austria should be postponed until the State Treaty had been signed and the occupying powers (the United States, France, the United Kingdom and the Soviet Union) had withdrawn.

Austria later expressed interest in sending observers to sessions of the Assembly, which responded in November 1951 by inviting it to do so, starting in 1952. In 1953, Austria was also authorised to send observers to meetings of some of the Council's intergovernmental committees.

In December 1953, several members of the Austrian National Council tabled a motion, asking the government to determine whether Austria was now eligible for Council of Europe membership. A similar initiative was taken in January 1956, when the Austrian State Treaty had been concluded, and permanent

Foundation and first members

■ **Raising of the Austrian flag,**
at the Council of Europe,
16 avril 1956.

In December 1953, several members of the Austrian National Council asked the government to determine whether Austria was eligible to join the Council of Europe. A similar initiative was taken in January 1956, when Austrian neutrality had been anchored in the Constitution. Hoping that the USSR might agree to reduce Austria's heavy financial obligations under the State Treaty, the government hesitated – particularly since an Austrian paper had reprinted an Izvestia article, attacking the Council as an enemy to the USSR and the peoples' democracies. Nonetheless, on 16 April 1956, Austria became the Council's fifteenth member state.

Austrian neutrality written into the Constitution. Fearing that its joining the Council would annoy the Soviets, with whom it hoped to negotiate a reduction in the heavy economic burden laid on Austria by the State Treaty, the government hesitated. Its doubts were reinforced by an *Izvestia* article, reprinted that month in the *Volksstimme*, which accused the Organisation of being hostile to the USSR and the peoples' democracies.

Nonetheless, the Austrian government and parliament decided to go for membership, considering – since the Council had no military brief – that neutrality was no obstacle. On 8 March 1956, the Committee of Ministers consulted the Assembly on admitting Austria. The Standing Committee, to which the question was referred, was quick to approve – although several members insisted that Austria (like Germany) must ratify the European Convention on Human Rights without delay.

On 16 April 1956, Austria became the Council's fifteenth member state, and its delegation, drawn from both houses of parliament, entered the Assembly. The members included Karl Czernetz, who went on to become President of the Assembly in 1975, and Lujo Toncic-Sorinj, who was elected Secretary General of the Council in 1969.

The delegation was welcomed by Fernand Dehousse, President of the Assembly, and Karl Wistrand, Chairman of the Special Committee on European Nations not represented in the Council, who said that this, the moment when the Council opened its arms to Austria and its people, was a solemn one.

Speaking for the Austrian delegation, Bruno Pittermann looked back to the time when Austria had been occupied and deprived of full sovereignty, and said that attending Assembly debates had provided *"great moral support"* and *"strengthened in us the conviction that the democratic states of Europe were following and sustaining with the utmost interest the struggle to safeguard human rights in Austria"*. He added: *"We wish to fulfil the mandate with which we have been entrusted and add our modest strength to yours so that, together, we may reach the goal to which we all aspire: to make Europe a continent in which peace is allied to freedom, and the home of human rights and contemporary humanism"*.

SWITZERLAND HANGS BACK

Switzerland – democratic, multicultural and wedded to the notion of popular sovereignty – seemed to have the makings of a model founder member.

Swiss neutrality, however, was an obstacle. In January 1949, the head of the Swiss diplomatic service was already telling French Foreign Minister Robert Schuman that his country was unwilling to join any political organisation or military alliance, although it did want economic co-operation with the rest of Europe. For this reason, Switzerland was not invited to join the Brussels Pact (later WEU) or the North Atlantic Treaty Organisation (NATO), or attend the preparatory meeting on establishing a European union (later the Council of Europe).

Switzerland could have been a founder member – but neutrality proved a problem.

Throughout the 1950s, Switzerland clung to its image of the Council as a highly politicised body. It is true that debates on foreign policy, and even European defence, were a permanent feature of the Assembly's agenda at that time. Nothing changed until May 1959, when the Assembly suggested that Swiss observers might follow its debates, and particularly those on economic issues. After some initial hesitation, the Swiss Government recommended, in May 1960, that Parliament send a delegation to observe these debates, without voting rights and with purely consultative status. This happened for the first time in March 1961, and worked so well that the Swiss Government and Parliament decided – since the Council was not a supranational organisation – that Switzerland could join without compromising its neutrality. It accordingly applied for membership in December 1962.

Swiss observers came to the Assembly for the first time in March 1961 – and the die was cast.

On 6 May 1963, Switzerland became a member. Welcoming its delegation the following day, Assembly President Pierre Pflimlin referred to *"the underlying relationship between the tradition of the Swiss Confederation and the spirit of our institution"*, and declared: *"The desire to be loyal to the ideal of freedom and safeguard democratic principles is also the essential characteristic of Switzerland, whose natural place among us was waiting to be filled. Its absence saddened us; now we can take comfort and be glad."*

The admission of these three countries was in line with the founding fathers' wish to make the Council all-embracing, excluding no country for cultural or religious reasons, and making no distinctions between victors and vanquished in the Second World War. This was why the Preamble to the Council's Statute had insisted on *"spiritual and moral values"* as *"the common heritage"* of Europe's peoples, and on the need for *"closer unity between all like-minded countries of Europe"*. It was this text, with its blend of political vision and openness, which underlay the Council's gradual extension to all the countries of western Europe, and later made it the first European institution to admit the newly democratic states of central and eastern Europe, once they had accepted the commitments embodied in the European Convention on Human Rights.

The founding fathers believed in open doors – no exclusion for cultural or religious reasons, and no distinctions between victors and vanquished.

■ **Pierre Pflimlin,**
President of the Parliamentary Assembly from 1963 to 1966.

An emblem for Europe: the Assembly chooses a flag

When the Council of Europe was founded, it was agreed that it would fly the member states' flags, in English alphabetical order.

At the time, many countries showed their commitment to Europe by flying two flags – their own, plus a European banner (for example the green "E" on a white background, adopted by the European Movement at The Hague Congress). The need for a universally accepted symbol began to make itself felt.

In August 1950, the Assembly's General Affairs Committee asked the Secretary General to produce a report on practical ways of publicising (and popularising) the European cause. It suggested that adopting a symbol should be the first step, and put its Committee on Rules of Procedure and Privileges to work on this question. Plans for a flag had been widely discussed, and the Council of Europe had already received over a hundred unsolicited proposals, including one from the European Parliamentary Union, which offered the use of its own flag. A first selection was made, and some 12 proposals were put to the Assembly in December 1951 – but none pleased everyone.

Salvador de Madariaga, President of the European Cultural Centre, came up with an independent idea. As an emblem of Europe (not just the Council), he suggested a blue flag with gold stars to mark the location of the continent's free capitals in 1938, plus a larger one for Strasbourg. The Assembly's members liked the colour combination – and the image of a star-sprinkled sky.

On 25 September 1953, in Resolution 41, it accordingly adopted as its flag 15 gold stars, none of them touching, arranged in a circle on an azure background – the circle to symbolise union, the stars standing for hope.

It urged the Committee of Ministers to adopt the same emblem for the Council of Europe as a whole, and *"instruct the Secretary General to enter into negotiations with the other European institutions to ensure that the emblems adopted by them shall have features similar to that adopted by the Council of Europe"*.

The number of stars remained an issue, however, particularly as the Council of Europe was likely to expand. The Committee of Ministers eventually suggested that the number be fixed and symbolic.

Foundation and first members

The blue flag, with its 12 gold stars, celebrated its 50th anniversary on 9 December 2005. For half a century, it has symbolised Europe's aspirations and achievements.

It was adopted in 1955 by the Council of Europe and its then 14 member states. In 1986, the European Communities (now the European Union) adopted the same flag.

Celebrations for the 50th anniversary of the European Flag,
Strasbourg,
16 November 2005.

In 1955, the Assembly chose between two proposals. The emblem adopted was a slight variation on the first design – *12 gold stars in a circle on an azure background*.

This flag was officially adopted by the Committee of Ministers on 8 December 1955.

Subsequently, the Assembly suggested more than once that adoption of the same symbol by the other European organisations would underline the unity of democratic Europe and the complementarity of its institutions.

In April 1983, the European Parliament took up this idea and suggested that the European Communities adopt the Council of Europe's emblem. Meeting in Milan in June 1985, the European Council accepted the proposal, feeling that this would help to give Europe and its people a clear visual identity at home and in the world at large. With the Council of Europe's agreement, the flag became the emblem of the European Communities in 1986.

Addressing the Assembly on 10 May 1990, Václav Havel, President of the Czech and Slovak Federal Republic, declared: *"To me, the 12 stars in your emblem do not express the proud conviction that the Council of Europe will build heaven on this earth. There will never be heaven on earth. I see these 12 stars as a reminder that the world could become a better place if, from time to time, we had the courage to look up at the stars."*

The European anthem

The search for a flag had elicited numerous proposals, and the news that the Council of Europe was looking for an anthem triggered much the same response.

The prime movers here were regional and local authorities, which were pleased with the flag, and now wanted an anthem to give their European festivals, celebrations and events an added touch of solemnity. The Assembly discussed the matter and decided, in 1971, that adopting an already well-known piece of music would be better than commissioning a new one.

In Resolution 492(1971), it noted that the time had come *"to choose an anthem for the European building"* and expressed its preference for *"a musical work representative of European genius"*, already in semi-traditional use on European occasions. The piece it had in mind was the *Ode to Joy* from the fourth movement of Beethoven's ninth symphony – a choice which most of its members had approved without demur.

The Committee of Ministers formally adopted the new anthem in 1972, and the Council of Europe asked the celebrated conductor, Herbert von Karajan, to provide three arrangements – for piano, wind instruments and orchestra. The anthem has no words, but its music's universal language eloquently conveys the European ideals of freedom, peace and solidarity.

The European Community leaders took a leaf from the Council of Europe's book at their meeting in Milan (June 1985), when they also adopted the "Ode to Joy" as their official anthem.

Shaping the new Europe

"The Consultative Assembly will provide a means through which the aspirations of the European peoples may be formulated and expressed, the governments thus being kept continuously in touch with European public opinion."

■ **Official Declaration, published when the Statute was signed,** 5 May 1949.

Shaping the new Europe

For some years, the Strasbourg Assembly remained Europe's only such body – and can well be seen as the matrix of the other European parliamentary institutions which came after it. Until the late 1950s, it served as the main parliamentary forum for discussion of Europe's future – and its immediate political problems.

Deeply aware of its responsibilities, and impelled by the dynamism of its members, who were already working heart-and-soul for Europe in their own countries, the Assembly set itself clear priorities: to prepare a political blueprint for Europe, launch a human rights convention as a moral and legal basis for that project, and preserve the Council of Europe's role in the face of new initiatives. It accordingly watched closely, as the European Coal and Steel Community (ECSC) and the European Economic Community (EEC) took shape, and suggested ways in which the Council could work with them.

Until the late 1950s, the Assembly was the main parliamentary forum for discussion of Europe's future – and its problems.

A POLITICAL AUTHORITY FOR EUROPE

As soon as the Assembly became operational, the Committee of Ministers asked it to consider changes in Europe's political structure which might be needed to forge closer ties between the Council of Europe's members and enable them to co-operate effectively in the areas listed in Article 1 of its Statute. The Assembly realised that the challenge was a major one – and showed this when it noted, in the debate on 6 September 1949, that it was being asked to do nothing less than to create a

"European political authority invested with limited functions but real powers". Its preparatory work on this took two years.

At this crucial juncture, when the two blocs which were destined to divide the continent for the next 50 years were emerging, there was no time to be lost.

In March 1947, France and the United Kingdom concluded a co-operation and assistance treaty in Dunkirk. The US Marshall Plan was also launched in 1947, and Moscow's veto on participation by the countries of central and eastern Europe drove the wedge between East and West a little deeper.

At the end of December 1947, the western countries agreed that a "western bloc" was needed, and extended the co-operation and assistance covered by the Treaty of Dunkirk to Belgium, the Netherlands and Luxembourg.

Speaking in the House of Commons in January 1948, Ernest Bevin, the United Kingdom Foreign Secretary, insisted that *"the question of associating other historic members of European civilisations"* with the new enterprise would have to be considered.

In April 1948, the Organisation for European Economic Co-operation (OEEC) was founded, mainly to co-ordinate Marshall Aid.

On 25 January 1949, Moscow responded to these moves towards intensified economic co-operation within Europe, and between Europe and the US, by setting up COMECON (Council for Mutual

The founding of COMECON was Moscow's response to increased economic co-operation in the West.

Shaping the new Europe

Economic Assistance) to control and organise its own sphere of economic influence. On 4 April, the Treaty of Washington established the North Atlantic Alliance.

The first major crisis came in May 1948, when the Soviet Union blockaded Berlin, and the western powers airlifted supplies into the beleaguered city. The Jessup-Malik Agreement, concluded at the United Nations in New York, brought a political solution just before the signing of the Council of Europe's Statute in London on 5 May 1949. The Council's emergence at this uneasy juncture in world affairs made it suspect in certain parts of eastern Europe, where it was decried as "NATO's ideological arm".

The Assembly declared that Europe's political future would depend on rebuilding its economy.

The international situation was complicated still further by the outbreak of the Korean War, prompting the western allies to take concerted action.

TOWARDS ECONOMIC UNION…

At its very first session in August 1949, the Assembly discussed the economic situation in Europe – a Europe devastated by the war and sustained at long range by Marshall Aid. Speaking in the debate on 16 August, French MP André Philip declared: *"The obvious conclusion is that European economic unification, the foundations of which at least we must lay during the next two to three years, if we wish to avoid the disaster which threatens us all, will not be achieved either by talks between experts or negotiations between sovereign states. Nothing will be accomplished unless we are able to set up a number of economic organisations, themselves co-ordinated by a European political authority capable of taking decisions by majority vote."*

… AND A EUROPEAN PARLIAMENT

André Philip went on to sketch a scenario in which the Council of Europe might become the institutional core of the European process, with an Assembly free to determine its own agenda and a Committee of Ministers which was not *"merely an assembly of diplomats, using their right of veto, which has already done too much harm in other international assemblies for any of us to wish to have it permanently here, but a real political authority ruling by majority, taking decisions and effectively responsible to the political assembly which we form and which is, after all, the nucleus, we hope, of what will become a European parliament"*. His words were prophetic. Europe would get its parliament, but it would not be the Strasbourg Assembly – although its pioneering role as the matrix of modern European parliamentarianism would not be forgotten.

After a stormy sitting, which ended at 2.45 a.m. on the night of 10/11 December 1951, the Assembly rejected the proposed European conference. This was a major blow to the many who had seen the Council of Europe as the first step towards a strong and integrated Europe. Paul-Henri Spaak resigned as President, declaring: "From time to time one feels in this Assembly as if one would like to be a little mad, to cast one's discretion and reason aside, to believe that, in order to build great things in this world, a little hope, a little confidence and a little faith achieve more than all the discretion of formal procedure."

Paul-Henri Spaak, President of the Assembly,
speaking in the Assembly Chamber,
10 December 1951.

THE COUNCIL OF EUROPE AND THE SCHUMAN PLAN

On 9 May 1950, French Foreign Minister Robert Schuman proposed setting up a European Coal and Steel Community (ECSC) – a supreme joint authority, controlling the coal and steel production of France, Germany, Belgium, the Netherlands and Luxembourg. On 10 August, he detailed his plan in the Council of Europe Assembly, which now included German delegates (Germany had become an associate member in July). The Treaty establishing the European Coal and Steel Community was duly signed in May 1951.

The Assembly found it relatively easy to agree on the Schuman plan, but planning Europe's future was a very different matter, and here the political rifts soon opened. Great Britain, looking first to its Commonwealth and its partnership with the US, was not over-interested in helping to build a Europe which the continental powers would inevitably dominate. France, for its part, was afraid that setting up a full-scale European political authority would effectively open the door to German rearmament.

Things came to a head in December 1951, when the Assembly had to vote on a recommendation calling for the co-ordination of European policy at the Council of Europe, the setting-up of a political authority and the holding of a European conference, early in 1952, to devise a coherent plan for the rational linking of specialised agencies, such as the ECSC, with the global European organisation embodied in the Council. The stumbling

The Assembly could agree on the Schuman plan – but planning Europe's future was a very different matter.

block was the suggestion that states prepared to join in setting up a political authority hold a select meeting alongside the conference.

LEADING POLITICIANS AT THE ASSEMBLY

The issue was crucial. Two heads of government, Alcide De Gasperi (Italy) and Konrad Adenauer (Germany), and two foreign ministers, Robert Schuman (France) and Paul van Zeeland (Belgium), threw themselves into the fray, urging the Assembly to be bold.

President Spaak declared: *"This is indeed a historic occasion which we have just witnessed. We have also this afternoon been witnesses of a historic fact; the ministers of France and Germany have come to lay a common policy before us. Between the two wars, two great statesmen, Mr Briand and Mr Stresemann, tried to achieve this co-operation. Let us remember, sadly, all the hardship and the sacrifices which the failure of their policy brought us! And now once more we are given the chance of reconciling ancient and long-standing European quarrels. The responsible ministers have come to ask our support in that momentous task. I should like to be able to assure Mr Schuman and Mr Adenauer that this Assembly, today, will not disappoint them."*

When he spoke, Chancellor Adenauer made urgency his keynote: *"There can be, for us, but one watchword: Let us act! Let us act quickly! Tomorrow it may be too late!"*

■ **Committee of Ministers session.**
*Left to right: Robert Schuman (France), Alcide De Gasperi (Italy), Dirk Stikker (Netherlands), Paul van Zeeland (Belgium), Konrad Adenauer (Germany) and Joseph Bech (Luxembourg),
Strasbourg,
December 1951.*

After a stormy sitting, which ended at 2.45 a.m. on the night of 10/11 December 1951, the Assembly accepted the other proposals, but rejected the European conference. This was a devastating blow to all those who had hoped that the Council of Europe would be the first step towards a strong and integrated Europe. Paul-Henri Spaak, who had nursed high hopes of Europe's first assembly, was among the hardest hit. He resigned as President, declaring: *"From time to time one feels in this Assembly as if one would like to be a little mad, to cast one's discretion and reason aside, to believe that, in order to build great things in this world, a little hope, a little confidence and a little faith achieve more than all the discretion of formal procedure."*

Nonetheless, the Assembly did not lose heart, but struck out in new directions. As its new President, it elected François de Menthon (France), a close wartime associate of General de Gaulle and a *Compagnon de la Libération*.

DEFENDING EUROPE

Defence was excluded from the Council of Europe's remit by its Statute, but that did not stop the Assembly from adopting (on 11 August 1950, at Winston Churchill's suggestion) a recommendation calling for the establishment of a European army, united under the command of a European defence minister and subject to democratic control. It also took an interest in the proposed European Defence Community (EDC) Treaty, covering

In a recommendation adopted in 1950, the Assembly called for a European army.

Shaping the new Europe

six Council countries (France, Italy, Germany, Belgium, the Netherlands and Luxembourg).

In 1952, it supported the EDC project as the best means of guaranteeing Europe's security, strengthening NATO and maintaining peace, insisting that it – and the forces placed under its command – must be genuinely European. It also stressed that the EDC should be subject to a political authority, which might be set up within the Council of Europe.

Another project it had to consider that year was the plan put forward in March by Anthony Eden, United Kingdom Foreign Secretary, for organic linking of the Council of Europe, the ECSC and the two communities which the "Six" (France, Germany, Italy, Belgium, Luxembourg and the Netherlands) were contemplating – one for defence (EDC), the other for political co-operation. The idea was to turn the Assembly into a body of variable geometry, acting as the parliamentary wing of the Council – and of these two communities as well.

To avoid partitioning Europe, Britain felt that it must be associated with the communities projected by the "Six", and the Assembly agreed. Discussion of these issues led, in 1953, to the holding of joint meetings of the Council of Europe and ECSC assemblies, usually in the Strasbourg Chamber.

The Assembly favoured UK involvement with the communities projected by the "Six" as a means of keeping Europe cohesive.

■ **Meeting at the Council of Europe.**
Left to right: Jean Monnet, President of the Supreme Authority of the ECSC, Guy Mollet, President of the Assembly, and Léon Marchal, Secretary General of the Council of Europe,
1954.

A JOINT EXTERNAL POLICY

Stalin's death in March 1953, and the slackening of international tension which followed it, prompted the Assembly to hold a general debate on "Definition of the policy of the Council of Europe in the light of recent developments in the international situation". On the basis of a report prepared by Paul-Henri Spaak, it adopted Resolution 44 of 26 September 1953, setting out – for the first time – a joint external policy for the Council's member states, and laying down principles to guide it.

It also proposed that the United States, the Soviet Union, France and the United Kingdom hold a further quadripartite meeting to discuss (principally) the Austrian and German questions, and listed the main issues which peace treaties with those two countries should cover.

Finally, it demonstrated its desire for peace by proposing the conclusion, at the UN, of a mutual security pact for Europe, covering the Soviet Union, the United States, the United Kingdom and France – and also the members of the future European political community.

On 20 May 1954, it elected as its President Guy Mollet (France), who had been a member since August 1949, and had chaired the General Affairs Committee from 1951 to 1954.

A POLITICAL FORUM FOR EUROPE

In August 1954, the French National Assembly voted against the EDC – also sounding the death knell of the proposed European Political Community. Within a month, French Prime Minister Pierre Mendès-France was reassuring the Assembly in Strasbourg that France still wanted close co-operation in Europe, based on Franco-German reconciliation. The project might have been shelved, but the great ideas behind it were still valid. As a ready-made alternative, he suggested recycling the Brussels Treaty of March 1948 and using it to consolidate peace and security in Europe. This would make it possible to involve Germany in joint defence (a prospect which had partly determined the National Assembly's rejection of the EDC). The main task under the revised Brussels Treaty would be limiting and controlling arms in western Europe. There would be no risk of overlapping with NATO, and links could be forged with the Council of Europe and the ECSC.

A few days later, the Assembly approved the proposed modification and geographical enlargement of the Brussels Treaty, including the administrative and technical integration of the European forces stationed on the continent, and control of arms manufacture. Going further than Mendès-France, it suggested that the revised treaty should provide for democratic supervision by a parliamentary assembly. In May 1955, the new Assembly of the revised WEU Treaty held its first meeting in Strasbourg. This is the Council of Europe Assembly's sister

French Prime Minister Pierre Mendès-France came to reassure the Assembly that his country still wanted close co-operation in Europe, based on Franco-German reconciliation.

institution for defence and security, and member states send the same delegations to both.

Germany's first turn to chair the Committee of Ministers came in May 1954, and the Assembly again welcomed Chancellor Konrad Adenauer. Focusing on East-West relations, he sent the countries of central and eastern Europe this message: *"It is true that the Council of Europe does not comprise all European states, but we desire and hope that all those who have not yet joined will also in time become members. We do not wish to continue without them in the long run, and indeed we cannot, and they must know that we are expecting them here."*

"The Council of Europe does not comprise all European states, but we desire and hope that all those who have not yet joined will also in time become members",
Konrad Adenauer, May 1954.

This question came up again a year later, when UK Foreign Secretary Harold Macmillan suggested in the Assembly, on 6 July 1955, that the Council of Europe should adopt a more open approach to other European states, and admit observers from countries like Yugoslavia. The Assembly and the Committee of Ministers discussed relations with Yugoslavia, and the possibility of associating it with certain Council activities on several occasions in the next few months. But the time was clearly not ripe, and the issue was not revived until the late 1960s.

In 1955, the European cause got a further boost when the foreign ministers of France, Italy, Germany, Belgium, the Netherlands and Luxembourg met in Messina (Italy) to devise a new framework for European economic co-operation. The Assembly accepted their conclusions, and urged its members to achieve a higher level of economic co-operation, mutual assistance and integration in

■ **Konrad Adenauer, Chancellor of the Federal Republic of Germany,**
Strasbourg,
May 1954.

western Europe. It suggested that convertible currencies, free trade, reduced customs tariffs and more rational use of agricultural resources held some of the keys to doing this.

COMMON MARKET AND EUROPEAN FREE TRADE AREA

Throughout 1956, the "Six" were working towards a common market, and the Assembly supported their efforts.

Following the signing of the Treaties of Rome – one establishing the European Economic Community (EEC) and the other the European Atomic Energy Community (Euratom) – in March 1957, the Assembly hailed the EEC as the most important step so far on the path to European unity. It hoped that a free trade area or some other arrangement would be introduced, making it easier to associate other Council of Europe member states with the common market. It also called for the harmonisation of social legislation, in consultation with workers and employers, and that the European Social Charter, which was then being prepared, should be taken into account. It later urged the need for close relations between the new European Communities and the Council of Europe, and between their assemblies, which were to share the same venue and continue to hold joint meetings.

To stop western Europe dividing, the Assembly pressed ahead with its proposals for a European free trade area, to include the EEC. Its debates on this crucial issue brought numerous ministers and state secretaries responsible for economics and trade to Strasbourg. The Convention establishing the European Free Trade Association (EFTA), of which Austria, Denmark, Iceland, Norway, Portugal, the United Kingdom, Sweden and Switzerland were members, was signed in Stockholm in 1960.

WILLY BRANDT AND THE STATUS OF BERLIN

In November 1958, the USSR notified the western powers that it regarded the agreements on the administration of Greater Berlin as null and void. It wanted negotiations with the West on demilitarising West Berlin and giving it "free city" status. It also delivered an ultimatum: if no agreement had been reached within six months, it would put its plan, which included obstructing communication with the West, into operation. The Assembly decided to hold a debate on the divided city's problems, and invited its mayor, Willy Brandt, to address it. Two federal German ministers also attended. Welcoming Willy Brandt, Assembly President Fernand Dehousse declared: *"Your place in history has been assured in your own lifetime; you have become the embodiment of a whole nation fighting for its existence and its freedom."*

Willy Brandt vehemently opposed any unilateral change in the status of Berlin, and insisted that the agreements between the allies, which guaranteed West Berlin the western powers'

In November 1958, the USSR denounced the agreements on the administration of Greater Berlin. The Assembly invited the city's mayor, Willy Brandt, to address it. He insisted that the city's status must not be altered unilaterally, and that the agreements concluded by the allies, guaranteeing West Berlin the western powers' protection, with full and free access, must be respected. The Assembly affirmed its solidarity with the city, and reminded the Soviet Union of their obligations to it.

Willy Brandt (right), Mayor of Berlin, in the Assembly, November 1958.

protection, with full and free access to the city, must be respected. The Assembly adopted a firm message of support, reminded the USSR in no uncertain terms of its obligations to Berlin, and recommended that the western powers lose no time in opening negotiations with the Soviet Union on the entire German problem.

AN AUDIENCE WITH GENERAL DE GAULLE

Between 1950 and 1960, the Assembly had two main priorities: to rationalise the European project and make it cohesive by linking the numerous initiatives launched at that time, and to assert the young Council of Europe's role as a global platform for European policy. Repeatedly, it called on the Committee of Ministers to keep the process focused, and on the member states to exploit the Council's full potential and the Ministers endorsed its position in Resolution (59) 11. Then, the Assembly decided in 1961 – when Danish MP Per Federspiel was President – to set up a "Working Party to re-activate the Council of Europe" which asked for a meeting with General Charles de Gaulle, President of the French Republic.

This meeting took place on 10 October 1961. The Assembly's delegation comprised its President, its French Vice-President, Emile Liquard, and the Working Party's Chairman, Auguste Pinton (France). One of its questions to the General was whether the Council of Europe would still have a role of its own, once the Common Market expanded. He replied that even an enlarged Common Market would remain confined to

The Assembly had two priorities: to bring order and cohesion to the European project, and assert the young Council of Europe's role as a global platform for European policy.

Shaping the new Europe

De Gaulle believed that an enlarged Common Market would remain confined to economics, and that ways of expressing "Europe's personality" in other areas would still be needed.

economics, and that ways of expressing "Europe's personality" in other areas would still have to be found, and major efforts made to forge closer ties between European countries, inside and outside the Common Market, in the cultural, social, legal and other spheres. All these countries were close in terms of outlook, lifestyle and economic level, and it was only natural that they should have a shared organisation to speak for them and express their values. "European personality" demanded specifically European forms of co-operation. All the free countries of the world must pull together, and Europe's sense of its own identity must not interfere with this – but Europe must also be able to speak freely for itself. The Council must try to make people aware of the things that made Europe what it was. The Working Party later met Chancellor Adenauer and the foreign ministers, Bruno Kreisky (Austria), Evangelos Averoff (Greece), Antonio Segni (Italy) and Edward Heath, then Lord Privy Seal (United Kingdom).

3

Making laws for Europe

> *"Every member of the Council of Europe must accept the principles of the rule of law and of the enjoyment by all persons within its jurisdiction of human rights and fundamental freedoms [...]."*

■ **Article 3 of the Statute of the Council of Europe.**

Making laws for Europe

The Council of Europe was not originally seen as working for European integration, and this was one of the reasons why its Statute gave the Assembly no law-making powers. The latter immediately realised, however, that the new European order needed legal foundations, and it put the Council on the standard-setting course it has firmly followed ever since. To that extent, the Assembly itself is a source of European law, even though it is the Committee of Ministers which formally adopts conventions and opens them for signature by the member states.

The Assembly made human rights its first priority, responding to the pressing demands voiced by the peoples of Europe and by The Hague Congress in May 1948.

HUMAN RIGHTS – AN URGENT ISSUE

Two world wars had resulted in the absolute negation of human dignity throughout Europe – a process which reached its nadir in the death camps. No surprise, then, that the Assembly made protecting human rights its first priority, responding to the pressing demands voiced by the peoples of Europe and by The Hague Congress in May 1948. At its very first session in August 1949, it urged the Committee of Ministers to *"cause a draft convention to be drawn up as early as possible, providing a collective guarantee, and designed to ensure the effective enjoyment by all persons residing within their territories of the rights and fundamental freedoms referred to in the Universal Declaration of Human Rights"*.

In his opening address, rapporteur Pierre-Henri Teitgen (France) declared: *"This fundamental affirmation is inscribed at the very foundation of our union: every man, by reason of his origin, his nature and his destiny, has certain indefeasible rights, against which no reason of state may prevail. And so, at our first meeting, we are opening a debate with the object of working out proposals which will enable Europe to fulfil its promise."*

Some Assembly members thought that the convention should list rights – civil, political, cultural, social and economic – as comprehensively as possible. The basic aim, however, was to get a binding text, backed by machinery to monitor compliance, with minimum delay. As a compromise, the Assembly agreed to select some ten political and civil rights from the Universal Declaration of Human Rights, and so provisionally dropped its proposal that social, economic and cultural rights be included.

It was soon accepted that the Convention for the Protection of Human Rights and Fundamental Freedoms – commonly known as the European Convention on Human Rights (ECHR) – would embody the Council of Europe's identity and aims in the human rights field, and underlie everything it did. From the very beginning, the Assembly also took the view that any state wishing to join the Council should be required to ratify the ECHR first.

The ECHR was adopted in Rome on 4 November 1950. At the ceremony during which the ECHR was opened for signature, Sir David Maxwell-Fyfe, Chairman of the Assembly's Legal Affairs Committee, said: *"Some may say that it is of doubtful value that the democratic nations should reinforce individual liberty among themselves and leave totalitarian states untouched. We do not accept this pessimistic view. We consider that our light will be a beacon to those at the moment in totalitarian darkness and will give them a hope of return to freedom."*

It was soon accepted that the Convention would embody the Council of Europe's identity and its aims in the human rights field – and underlie everything it did.

Making laws for Europe

The only tribunal of its kind in the world, the European Court of Human Rights can compel states to respect its judgments.

The Convention was the first major post-war standard-setting instrument submitted for ratification to west European parliaments. It came into force within three years, on 3 September 1953. The European Court of Human Rights, with judges elected by the Assembly, was formally established to monitor compliance on 18 September 1959.

The Assembly was subsequently involved in preparation of all the protocols which later extended the list of rights protected. These included Protocol No. 1, which guarantees the holding of free and secret elections at regular intervals, Protocols Nos. 6 and 15 on abolition of the death penalty, and Protocol No. 12, which embodies a general ban on discrimination. The right of direct individual petition, allowing anyone to bring a defaulting state before the Court, was also introduced at its prompting in 1998. The Court, which is the only tribunal of its kind in the world, has power to find states guilty of breaching the Convention, and its judgments are fully enforceable. The Committee of Ministers has the task of ensuring that they are executed and, in particular, that sums awarded in compensation are actually paid. The Assembly put the finishing touch to the machinery in 1999, when it introduced political monitoring of compliance with judgments. Its public debates are undoubtedly a useful source of pressure, encouraging offending states to pay compensation promptly and bring their laws into line with the Court's case law.

A SOCIAL CHARTER FOR EUROPE

As we have seen, some Assembly members had wanted to include social and economic rights in the ECHR. Ostensibly, they lost the argument – but the Assembly at once started working on a separate instrument to protect those rights too.

In a 1953 opinion (No. 5) for the Committee of Ministers, presented by the Belgian rapporteur Henri Heyman, the Assembly declared that the future European Social Charter *"should define the social aims of the member states and serve as a guide for all future activities of the Council in the social field. In social policy, it should form a pendant to the Convention on Human Rights and Fundamental Freedoms, and should be framed in agreement with the Assembly, whose function it should be to lay down the governing principles on which it should be based"*.

The Assembly's contribution to preparation of the Charter was decisive. In an effort to find compromise solutions and keep the project on track, in spite of disagreements with the Committee of Ministers, it produced five reports and three opinions. It authored several drafts itself, and suggested numerous amendments to the final one. The Charter's recognition of the right to strike, the aim of full employment and the right to social services were the fruit of its efforts. It also secured the setting-up of a labour inspection system, monitoring of compliance with the Charter, and the taking of decisions by a two-thirds majority of the Committee of Ministers.

Human rights were the Assembly's first concern. At its opening session, it called for a "collective guarantee of human rights", with a monitoring body to enforce it. The result was the Convention for the Protection of Human Rights and Fundamental Freedoms, signed in Rome on 4 November 1950. The Assembly elected the first judges to the European Court of Human Rights on 21 January 1959. On that same day, the Court's first President, Lord McNair (United Kingdom) was sworn in before the Assembly and its President, Fernand Dehousse (Belgium). One of the 14 other judges was René Cassin (France), the Court's Vice-President and a future winner of the Nobel Peace Prize.

Election of the first judges to the European Court of Human Rights, *in the Assembly Chamber, 21 January 1959.*

The Committee of Ministers did not, however, accept its proposals on acceptance of a "hard core" of guaranteed rights, maximum weekly working hours and family reunion – or its proposal for compulsory monitoring by a body like the European Court of Human Rights. It was finally decided that contracting states would submit regular reports on action taken to implement the Charter to the Secretary General, and that their compliance would be assessed on this basis.

Signed in Turin on 18 October 1961, the European Social Charter was intended to become – with the ECHR – one of the Council of Europe's main supporting pillars.

The Assembly continued to propose new ways of supplementing and strengthening the text. One of its ideas – in 1956 – was appointment of a Council of Europe social affairs commissioner. Another was attachment of a social chamber to the European Court of Human Rights.

A third suggestion, in 1978, was a collective complaints system – eventually introduced by a protocol opened for signing in Strasbourg on 9 November 1995. Later, to forestall the emergence of a "two-speed social Europe", the Assembly proposed that the European Community accede to the Charter.

Texts like the Charter obviously need to keep pace with changing requirements, and this was the subject of the comprehensive report on the future of the text, submitted in September 1991 by Italian MP Franco Foschi, who proposed revising it. This, and other Assembly reports making the same point, finally convinced

Thanks to the Assembly, the right to strike, the aim of full employment and the right to social services were written into the Charter.

the Committee of Ministers, and a revised text was opened for signing in 1996. This recognises new rights, including the right to protection against poverty and social exclusion, the right to housing, protection against harassment, including sexual harassment, and protection in cases of job loss.

Seven years later, the Assembly came up with new proposals, for example a European court of social rights, a complaints procedure for individuals, and compulsory acceptance by states of all the Charter's core articles.

Finally, in 2004, the Assembly asked the Committee of Ministers to give binding force to the five principles for satisfaction of the basic material needs of persons in situations of extreme poverty, which they duly did in Recommendation No. R (2000) 3.

Despite its shortcomings, particularly in the matter of monitoring, the European Social Charter forms the basis of European social policy on employment, education, social cohesion, the right to social and medical assistance, and protection of children, women and migrant workers. Moreover, it expressly recognises the right to strike. It got a new lease of life when the Iron Curtain went, and the Assembly made acceptance of the Charter a condition for central and east European states wishing to join the Council of Europe. Reflecting new labour market and social trends, the revised Charter introduces new rights, and now serves as a blueprint for the reform of national legislation and the harmonisation of social law in Europe.

> The European Social Charter forms the basis of European social policy on employment, education, social cohesion and the right to social and medical assistance.

■ **Pierre Laroque (right), first Chairman of the Committee of Independent Experts of the Social Charter, and Louis Jung, President of the Assembly, on the occasion of the Charter's 25th anniversary,**
Strasbourg,
19 November 1986.

CULTURE – A FORCE FOR UNITY

From the very beginning, the Assembly saw cultural co-operation as one of the keys to rebuilding Europe, healing divisions and securing peace for the future. The aim was to foster mutual understanding, based on shared values, but also on knowledge of others and respect for diversity.

At the Assembly's sitting on 26 August 1949, the issues were admirably stated by a French parliamentarian of African origin – Senegal's Léopold Sédar Senghor, who later became his country's first President, when it achieved independence in 1960.

Outlining the aims of the future cultural convention, he declared: *"An essential task of our Assembly is to define the common heritage of Europe, and to maintain that it is, primarily, a cultural heritage. The common heritage of Europe is the culture which was produced by grafting Christianity onto Greek logic. I say Christianity but, as you know, Islam is Christianity's brother in spirit and in origin. You are aware of the important part played by Islam in transmitting the heritage of Greece. I say Christianity but, as you know, Socialism is only a reaction of Christian origin against deviations from Christianity. The common heritage of Europe resides less in technical devices which have been exported to the furthest confines of the earth, and have become matters of common knowledge, than in that precision of method, by which Europe has succeeded in subjugating matter and controlling the blind forces of nature. The common heritage of Europe is the ideal of man which has been patiently built up and perfected during the course of twenty centuries. It is this ideal of man which will prevent the European in his turn from* being dominated by matter, that is, from being mastered by his own inventions, and so sharing the fate of the Sorcerer's Apprentice."

The general preamble to Recommendation 24 on cultural conventions, and other recommendations on cultural questions which the Assembly adopted in 1949, makes some profound and still very relevant points:

"European culture has its sources in the thought and work of free peoples based on centuries of tradition. It is one and varied. Its variety is derived from its origin. The differences in the structure and living conditions of nations are reflected in it, as are the many forms of free collective effort from which it comes. Generations of men and women of all social classes have left their mark on it. It is one in its respect for the human person, for the supremacy of the spirit, for freedom of opinion and the unfettered expression of ideas; in its uncompromising opposition to every form of tyranny. It is in the service of men and not of any one nation or class. No national or ideological consideration may prevail against it. No power can be allowed to prohibit or impede the individual search for truth. Culture cannot be regarded as an instrument of production. It cannot be measured by the technical progress which it permits, nor by the resulting increase in power. It is embodied essentially in the disinterested search for knowledge and in a flowering of personal qualities, which may assume the most elevated or the most humble form according to the individuals concerned. Culture must not be the privilege of a minority. Every man is entitled to it, just as he is to freedom, and it is the duty of every democracy to ensure access to it for each of its citizens, irrespective of economic and social inequalities."

"European culture has its sources in the thought and work of free peoples based on centuries of tradition. It is one and varied. Its variety is derived from its origin." Preamble to Recommendation 24, 1949.

Opened for signing on 19 December 1954, the European Cultural Convention rapidly became one of the Council of Europe's most successful texts.

The European Cultural Convention was opened for signing by the Council of Europe's then fourteen member states in Paris on 19 December 1954 – and rapidly became one of the Organisation's most effective and useful texts.

It had one totally new feature: it was open to non-member states, allowing them to participate in the Council of Europe's cultural activities on the same footing as members. In effect, it extended a hand to states held back from joining the Council by geopolitical factors, and associated them with a vast range of cultural activities, covering heritage, education, cultural identity and free circulation of values and ideas.

Thus, Spain and Finland acceded to the convention in 1957 and 1970 – but did not join the Council of Europe until 1977 and 1989 respectively. The Holy See acceded in 1962, and has worked closely with the Council ever since. Yugoslavia came on board in 1987, and all the states which have joined the Council since 1989 have accepted the European Cultural Convention first. Indeed, its usefulness in broadening the Council of Europe's range of contacts prompted the Assembly to ask the Committee of Ministers to extend it to some non-European countries as well, e.g. Canada, Israel and the countries of the Maghreb.

The European Cultural Convention undoubtedly embodies the vision of the founding fathers, who saw culture as the first, essential key to European unity. Without political strings, and in a highly practical way, it has forged ties and facilitated cultural exchange with countries which would otherwise have had no stake in the European project.

■ **Léopold Sédar Senghor,** *addressing the Assembly, 26 August 1949.*

From the start, the Assembly saw cultural co-operation as a key to rebuilding Europe. The aim was to foster mutual understanding, based on shared values, but also on knowledge of others and respect for diversity. Léopold Sédar Senghor, a French MP of African origin, and later President of Senegal, put it well in the Assembly on 26 August 1949. Speaking of the aims of the future cultural convention, he declared: "An essential task of our Assembly is to define the common heritage of Europe, and to maintain that it is, primarily, a cultural heritage."

TORTURE BAN

Prohibiting torture was one of the issues already covered by Pierre-Henri Teitgen's 1949 report for the Assembly on collective guarantees for essential freedoms and fundamental rights: *"No one shall be subjected to torture or to inhuman or degrading treatment or punishment"* – words which were later used in Article 3 of the European Convention on Human Rights. That same year, the Assembly solemnly declared that *"any use of torture by public authorities or individuals is a crime against humanity. It can never be justified even to extract information, to save life or to protect the interests of the state on any grounds whatsoever"*.

However, nothing more was done until the 1970s, when the UN launched a major anti-torture campaign, culminating in the adoption of a solemn declaration. Amnesty International supported its efforts and was vigorously active in the same cause. At the Council of Europe, the Assembly held a debate on torture in the world in October 1975. It insisted on the need for stronger anti-torture measures, and suggested that prohibiting extradition to countries suspected of using it, and refusing them legal assistance, should be the first step. The idea of setting up special machinery to prevent torture was floated in the debate. The Assembly was thinking in terms of a parliamentary committee of enquiry – but it realised that there might be overlapping with the European Convention on Human Rights, and that governments might be reluctant to admit a committee of this kind to their territory. Nonetheless, the idea of preventive action was now on the table, and support for it increased as time went on. Six years later, in 1981, the Assembly suggested that a UN convention, providing for regular, unannounced inspection of places of detention, would contribute effectively to preventing torture. Shortly afterwards, its Legal Affairs Committee, which feared that such a system was unlikely to materialise quickly at world level, proposed that Europe should take the lead itself. The committee's chairman, Senator Noël Berrier (France) wondered whether the European countries might not *"set an example and establish a system of this kind among themselves within the Council of Europe, without waiting for the project to be carried out at world level"*. He made the point that a system of this kind would be *"a useful adjunct to the measures which are available within the Council of Europe for combating torture, but only when the detainee has become a victim of torture"*.

In September 1983, the Assembly adopted Recommendation 971, containing a draft convention on the protection of persons deprived of their liberty against torture and cruel, inhuman or degrading punishment or treatment. This provided for regular, unannounced visits to places of detention. To make the system work, it took the unprecedented step of setting up a committee of independent experts with authority to inspect all places of confinement – prisons, police stations and mental hospitals – where people are held by the authorities.

The European Convention for the Prevention of Torture and Inhuman or Degrading Treatment or Punishment was opened for signature in November 1987. It came into force in 1989, just before the Council of Europe opened its doors to the new central and east European democracies. Very soon, the Assembly made promising to ratify it compulsory for states wishing to join the Council, and conditions of detention in member states have improved substantially

■ **Marcelo Palacios,**
Rapporteur of the Committee on Science and Technology,
1995.

as a result. There was one disappointment, however: the Assembly wanted to elect the members of the inspecting committee itself (it felt that this would increase their authority and guarantee their independence), but this proposal was rejected.

HUMAN RIGHTS AND BIOMEDICINE

The Assembly also made a pioneering contribution to preparation of the Convention on Human Rights and Biomedicine, which provoked intense discussion and led to a clash with the Committee of Ministers, whose draft it refused to accept without revision.

The Assembly started work on this question in the early 1980s, adopting recommendations on genetic engineering (1982), the use of human embryos and foetuses for diagnostic, therapeutic, scientific, industrial and commercial purposes (1986), and the use of human embryos and foetuses in scientific research (1989).

In these texts, it called for a European agreement, or at least a set of principles and guidelines. In June 1990, the Conference of European Ministers of Justice approved the preparation of a convention, and the Committee of Ministers submitted a draft to the Assembly for opinion in 1994.

The draft text aroused great interest among specialists, parliaments, churches and the public. It was declassified to permit broad public discussion, and the Assembly Secretariat was deluged with letters from individuals – most of them asking for a text which would give human dignity a high level of protection.

The European Convention for the Prevention of Torture and Inhuman or Degrading Treatment or Punishment came into force in 1989. Very soon, the Assembly made ratifying it a condition of Council of Europe membership.

The Assembly itself was divided. The Committee on Science and Technology, which was asked to decide on the substance of the text, was largely favourable. However, the Committee on Legal Affairs and Human Rights, which was also asked to give an opinion, had serious misgivings, chiefly concerning research on persons legally unable to consent, organ transplants and embryo research. After a stormy debate in September 1994, the Assembly asked the two committees to reconsider the text. A further debate was held in January 1995, on the basis of a report presented for the Committee on Science and Technology by Spanish MP Marcelo Palacios, and an opinion from the Committee on Legal Affairs and Human Rights, whose rapporteur was Austrian MP Walter Schwimmer, elected Secretary General of the Council of Europe in September 1999. In Opinion No. 184 (1995), the Assembly asked the Committee of Ministers to make substantial changes in the draft text.

In June 1996, the Committee of Ministers came up with a new draft. This met most of the objections raised by the Assembly, which acknowledged that it was coherent, balanced – and as close as possible to embodying a full European consensus.

The product of effective co-operation between the Committee of Ministers and the Assembly, the convention was the first binding international agreement in this field. It was finally opened for signing in 1997 at Oviedo (Spain). Protocols on the cloning of human beings (prohibited), human organ and tissue transplants, and biomedical research – all shaped in part by the Assembly's comments – were added later.

Making laws for Europe

The European Convention for the Prevention of Torture and Inhuman or Degrading Treatment or Punishment was opened for signing in November 1987, and came into force in 1989 – just before the Council of Europe opened its doors to the new central and east European democracies. It included one major innovation: a committee of independent experts empowered to inspect any facility – prisons, police stations or mental hospitals – where people are held by the authorities.

Exercise yard of a prison inspected by the CPT ■

■ **José Manuel Romay Beccaria, Spanish Minister of Health, signs the Convention on Human Rights and Biomedicine, under the gaze of Council of Europe Secretary General Daniel Tarschys,**
Oviedo (Spain),
4 April 1997.

Standard-setting dynamo

The Council of Europe has adopted some 200 treaties, all focused in a general sense on promoting the rule of law and human rights. They add up to an impressive body of European standards, and the Assembly has had a major hand in many of them, helping to get such basic Council texts as the European Convention on Human Rights, the European Social Charter and the European Cultural Convention safely off the ground.

From the very beginning, the Assembly has insisted on its standard-setting role, and its recommendations have inspired over a third of the Council of Europe's conventions. Sometimes – particularly when governments have been slow to act, and have needed pushing – it has come close to making laws itself, even preparing full drafts of certain conventions (soft law).

This happened in 1960, for example, when it authored a draft protocol to the European Convention on Human Rights, prohibiting discrimination *"on any grounds such as sex, race, colour, language, religion, political or other opinion, national or social origin, association with a national minority, property, birth or other status"*.

It did much the same in Recommendation 1201 (1993), which asked the Committee of Ministers to prepare a convention on the protection of minorities – something which some Assembly members had hoped to see included in the ECHR, when it was adopted in 1950.

The Assembly may lack the law-making powers of national parliaments – but it still plays a vital role by proposing new conventions when it feels they are needed, and encouraging states to sign and ratify existing ones.

4

No to capital punishment

> *"The death penalty shall be abolished. No one shall be condemned to such penalty or executed."*

■ Article 1 of Protocol No. 13 to the ECHR, concerning the abolition of the death penalty in all circumstances.

The Assembly is convinced that the European Convention on Human Rights must be flexible, and able to incorporate – via protocols – rights proposed but omitted at the start, and also new rights engendered by social, scientific and technical change. Its own efforts to get prohibition of the death penalty inserted date back to the early 1970s.

When the Convention was adopted in 1950, most of the Council of Europe's founder members still had capital punishment in theory, though some had stopped enforcing it in practice. Executions were still current in France, Greece, Ireland, Turkey and the United Kingdom.

When the ECHR was adopted in 1950, most of the Council of Europe's member states still had the death penalty.

The Nuremberg Tribunal, established immediately after the Second World War to try the Nazi leaders in the name of the democracies, had sentenced some of them to death, and the sentences had been carried out – which showed that politicians and the public still thought the death penalty appropriate for unusually heinous and barbaric crimes.

LEGALITY OF THE DEATH PENALTY

Against this background, there was nothing strange in the ECHR's confirmation that capital punishment was acceptable in law-governed states. Article 2, paragraph 1, of the chapter on "Rights and freedoms" is aware of no self-contradiction when it proclaims that *"everyone's right to life shall be protected by law"* and in the same breath continues *"no one shall be deprived of his life intentionally save in the execution of a sentence of a court following his conviction of a crime for which this penalty is provided by law"*. In other words, the death penalty is lawful.

The next paragraph goes even further, specifying cases in which non-judicial killing is allowable under the Convention. *"Deprivation of life shall not be regarded as inflicted in contravention of this article when it results from the use of force which is no more than is absolutely necessary: in defence of any person from unlawful violence; in order to effect a lawful arrest or to prevent the escape of a person lawfully detained; in action lawfully taken for the purpose of quelling a riot or insurrection."*

For over 30 years, this remained the situation.

THE BATTLE BEGINS

In the early 1970s, various Assembly members (many of them Scandinavian) were already campaigning against the death penalty in their own countries, and they raised the wider question of its continued existence in Europe at the Council.

The first motion for a resolution on abolition was tabled in the Assembly in 1973.

Prompted by the UK House of Commons' decision not to bring back the death penalty, Swedish MP Astrid Bergegren appealed to member states which still had it to wipe it from their statute books.

The first motion for a resolution on abolition was tabled in the Assembly in 1973.

The battle had begun, but was to prove a long one.

In fact, abolitionists were very much in the minority, and the Assembly hesitated. In January 1975, after lengthy discussion, its Legal Affairs Committee refused to submit a report on the question – a decision confirmed four months later by the Assembly, when it struck the issue from its agenda. Another Swedish MP, Henrik Lidgard (Labour), tried – unsuccessfully – to revive the debate, and resigned from the committee in January 1976.

THE ETHICAL ANGLE

The issue remained a dead letter until 1979, when yet another Swede, Carl Lidbom, submitted his report on abolition to the Assembly. Enlisting some of Europe's great thinkers in the cause, he quoted French writer Albert Camus (*"In the united Europe of tomorrow, formal abolition of capital punishment should be the first article of the European Code for which we all hope"*) and eighteenth-century Italian jurist Cesare Beccaria (*"What is this right whereby men presume to slaughter their fellows?"*).

When the Legal Affairs Committee met on 18 March 1980, the rapporteur pointed out that the political background to the debate had changed significantly in the space of a few years. Three of the states which had joined the Council of Europe in the meantime – Portugal, Spain and Liechtenstein – were against the death penalty. Moreover, the United Kingdom had

■ **Carl Lidbom,**
speaking at the Council of Europe,
1979.

No to capital punishment

■ **Robert Badinter, French Minister of Justice,** *addressing the Assembly,* 2 October 1981.

Protocol No. 6 to the ECHR, concerning the abolition of the death penalty, was opened for signature by the member states on 28 April 1983. Its first article contains just two sentences: "The death penalty shall be abolished. No one shall be condemned to such penalty or executed." *The abolitionist cause was greatly strengthened when France, the Council of Europe's host country, did away with the death penalty on 17 September 1981.* "That chapter is now closed", *declared French Minister of Justice Robert Badinter, speaking before the Assembly on 2 October 1981.*

restricted its use, and Sweden had abolished it. The UN, too, had shifted its ground (although most of its members still had capital punishment) and was no longer neutral, but openly in favour of abolition.

ABOLITION

The Assembly was now convinced that the traditional attitude reflected in Article 2 of the ECHR was no longer a viable option for the Council of Europe. In Resolution 727, adopted on 22 April 1980, it accordingly appealed *"to the parliaments of those member states of the Council of Europe, which have retained capital punishment for crimes committed in times of peace, to abolish it from their penal systems"*. Denouncing the death penalty as inhuman, it urged the Committee of Ministers to prepare a protocol to the ECHR, banning it in peacetime.

Capital punishment was now on the way out, and Protocol No. 6 concerning abolition of the death penalty was opened for signature in Strasbourg on 28 April 1983. Its first article is brief and to the point: *"The death penalty shall be abolished. No one shall be condemned to such penalty or executed."* The fact that France, the Council of Europe's host country, had come over, and abolished the death penalty on 17 September 1981, had done much to strengthen the abolitionist cause.

However, the Protocol did not go all the way, declaring, in Article 2, that *"a state may make provision in its law for the death penalty in respect of acts committed in time of war or of imminent threat of war"*. Obviously, the Assembly could not accept this situation for long – but a new problem needed solving first.

Once the Berlin Wall had gone (November 1989), and the USSR had been dismantled (December 1991), the emergent democracies in central and eastern Europe started queuing up to join the Council of Europe. This was clear and welcome confirmation that the Council's work for democracy, the rule of law and liberty throughout the continent still acted as a magnet, but capital punishment – not only the law, but widely enforced in the applicant countries – again became a problem.

MEMBERSHIP – A NEW CONDITION

A major principle was at stake, and the Assembly decided that its power to veto admissions (since 1951, the Committee of Ministers had needed its approval to admit new members) could be used to enforce it. On the strength of a report by Hans Göran Franck (Swedish again), it adopted Resolution 1044 (1994), making abolition of capital punishment an essential condition of membership, and insisting that candidate countries must halt executions forthwith, and commit themselves to signing Protocol No. 6 within three years.

This approach worked, though it sometimes caused problems for countries caught up in a radical process of transition, where public opinion – already shaken by the breakneck pace of political and economic change – was reluctant to let the death penalty go.

No to capital punishment

At the close of the 2nd Summit of Heads of State and Government of the Council of Europe, Europe's leaders ordered an immediate moratorium on executions in the few European countries which were still enforcing the death penalty, and called for its universal abolition. In a message to countries which still had death-row prisoners, the Assembly declared: "These member states must realise that the Assembly is unwilling to reconsider their commitments with regard to the abolition of the death penalty." Its words went home, and capital punishment in peacetime was a thing of the past in greater Europe when it entered the third millennium.

Line-up of leaders at the 2nd Summit, *Strasbourg,* 10-11 October 1997.

However, the Assembly got what it wanted, and none of the applicant countries ultimately jibbed at making the effort required of it. In practice and in law, they all did away with capital punishment, as the Committee on Legal Affairs and Human Rights noted with satisfaction on 8 April 1999.

In the meantime, Europe's leaders – meeting in Strasbourg on 10 and 11 October 1997, for the 2nd Summit of Heads of State and Government of the Council of Europe – had given the Council's position backing at the highest level, by insisting that the few European countries which were still enforcing the death penalty must respect an immediate moratorium, and calling for universal abolition.

In Resolution 1187 (1999), the Assembly sent countries which still had death-row prisoners an unequivocal message: *"These member states must realise that the Assembly is unwilling to reconsider their commitments with regard to the abolition of the death penalty. On the contrary, the Assembly will use all means at its disposal to ensure that commitments freely entered into are honoured."*

Its words went home, and capital punishment in peacetime was a thing of the past in greater Europe when it entered the third millennium.

In Resolution 1044 (1994), the Assembly made abolition of the death penalty an essential condition for joining the Council of Europe.

WARTIME TOO

The question of capital punishment in wartime – already raised by the Assembly in Resolution 1044 (1994) – still needed answering, however. In Opinion No. 233, presented in January 2002 by Liechtenstein MP Renate Wohlwend, the Assembly threw its full weight behind the proposal that capital punishment be totally – and unconditionally – abolished in Council of Europe member states. This was duly done when Protocol No. 13 to the ECHR, concerning abolition of the death penalty in all circumstances, was opened for signing in Vilnius on 3 May that year. The Council's work on the question was now complete – and the death penalty outlawed.

Thanks to the efforts of the Council of Europe (and the EU, which took up its work on human rights), Europe, the first continent without the death penalty, has not only pioneered abolition on its home ground, but is also campaigning actively to make the ban worldwide.

> Thanks to the Council of Europe and the EU, Europe has not only pioneered abolition of the death penalty on its home ground, but is also campaigning to make the ban worldwide.

■ **The European Court of Human Rights,**
Strasbourg.
Article 2, paragraph 1, of the European Convention on Human Rights, which was signed in Rome on 4 November 1950 and came into force on 3 September 1953, declares that: "Everyone's right to life shall be protected by law."

The next stage

The Assembly has not closed the file on abolition. The death penalty may have gone in the Council of Europe's 46 member states, but two observer countries – Japan and the US – still have it.

This situation is unacceptable for the Assembly which said so clearly in Resolution 1253, adopted on 25 June 2001: *"When Japan and the United States were granted observer status with the Council of Europe, the Organisation's position on capital punishment was already clear, but had not yet been taken on board by all European states. Today, the Council of Europe does not accept countries in its midst which carry out executions. Viewing the application of the death penalty as a violation of the most fundamental human rights, such as the right to life and the right to be protected against torture and inhuman or degrading treatment, the Assembly thus finds Japan and the United States in violation of their obligations under Statutory Resolution (93) 26."*

Dialogue with parliamentarians in both these countries is now under way, and there are hopes of a positive outcome. There have recently been encouraging signs from the US Supreme Court, which has twice restricted use of the death penalty, declaring executions of disabled or under-age offenders unconstitutional.

In Japan, too, attitudes are changing, and the Assembly is engaged in promising dialogue with the Parliamentary League for Abolition of the Death Penalty and the Japanese Federation of Bar Associations.

Goal – universal abolition

At the 1st World Congress against the Death Penalty, in Strasbourg on 22 June 2001, the Presidents of the Parliamentary Assembly and the European Parliament, Lord Russell-Johnston and Nicole Fontaine, and the presidents of 13 national parliaments, solemnly called for an immediate, worldwide *"moratorium on executions of those sentenced to death"*.

They went on: *"We are convinced that the death penalty is a violation of the most fundamental of human rights – the right to life, which is recognised by regional and international human rights instruments. Since its application is irreversible, since no criminal justice system can rule out the risk of condemning innocent people, since, moreover, it is often applied in a discriminatory manner, and since there is no evidence that this penalty is a more effective deterrent than others, we consider that the death penalty is an inadequate form of punishment, especially if there are ways of combating serious crime without failing to respect human rights.*

We support the large-scale movement in favour of abolishing this penalty, which has led to its elimination in more than half the countries of the world. Europe has shown the utmost determination in supporting this cause.

Convinced that the worldwide abolition of the death penalty would be a vital contribution to ensuring respect for human dignity and human rights, we call on all states to introduce a worldwide moratorium on executions without delay, and to take steps to abolish the death penalty in their domestic law."

■ **First World Congress against the Death Penalty**
(centre, Lord Russell-Johnston, President of the Parliamentary Assembly,
Mrs Nicole Fontaine, President of the European Parliament),
Strasbourg,
22 June 2001.

5. The Mediterranean dimension

"The Europe in which we believe is the Europe of freedoms. Its states must co-ordinate their policies closely, since, while there are some who think it too big to live united, I believe it too small to live divided."

■ **Adolfo Suárez, Head of Spain's first post-Franco government,** *speaking in the Assembly,* 31 January 1979.

The Mediterranean dimension

> In the 1960s, the Council of Europe was the first institution to welcome two newly independent Mediterranean states, and help them to achieve democratic stability.

ADMITTING NEW STATES, DEFENDING OLD PRINCIPLES

With France and Italy among its founder members, the Council of Europe had a Mediterranean dimension from the outset, and the Committee of Ministers strengthened it at its very first meeting (8 August 1949) by inviting Greece and Turkey to join – with the result that parliamentarians from both were present a day later at the Assembly's solemn opening session.

The Committee's decision on admitting Greece and Turkey raised issues already hotly debated at the London Ministerial Conference in May, where consensus had taken some reaching. The intention had been to make the new organisation as homogeneous as possible, and some participants had suggested that discrepancies in democratic standards between those two countries and the founder members might tell against this. Geopolitics carried the day, however. Greece had invented democracy, and so there was a natural desire to bind it firmly to democratic Europe, while Turkey's membership of the Organisation for European Economic Co-operation (OEEC) had already given it an acknowledged European role. Finally, it had been agreed that bringing them in was better than leaving them outside – and would expose them to the Council of Europe's positive influence. Later, in the 1960s, the Council became the first institution to welcome two newly independent Mediterranean states – Cyprus, which joined in 1961, and Malta, which joined in 1965 – and help them to achieve democratic stability.

Europe, Asia and Africa meet on the Mediterranean, and this makes it a focus for contact and exchange – but also for conflicting influences and tensions, which are not easily, or always successfully, managed.

There is nothing to regret in Malta's case, but – in spite of the Assembly's recent decision to invite elected representatives of the Turkish Cypriot community to participate in its work – the Cyprus conflict has yet to be fairly and durably resolved.

When crises hit Greece and Turkey, in 1967 and 1980 respectively, it was the Assembly which stood up for the Council of Europe's principles. In the same way, its initiatives and its contacts with democratic organisations in Portugal and Spain helped to forge links with those countries, which were ruled by dictators for a quarter of a century. Things changed in Portugal with the "Carnation Revolution" in April 1974, and in Spain when Franco died in 1975. The first joined the Council in 1976, and the second in 1977. A memorable moment came at the Assembly's plenary sitting on 12 October 1977, when a delegation from the Spanish Cortès gave a solemn undertaking that their country would honour the Council's ideals and respect human rights.

The Organisation acquired its present Mediterranean dimension when Monaco joined on 5 October 2004.

Portugal joined the Council of Europe in 1976, once the 1974 "Carnation Revolution" had opened the way to membership. After Franco's death in 1975, Spain followed suit in 1977.

CRISIS IN GREECE

On 21 April 1967, the Council of Europe found itself facing a major crisis in one of its oldest member states.

The Mediterranean dimension

Fearing a left-wing election victory, the "Colonels" – Nicolas Makarezos, Georgios Papadopoulos and Stylianos Patakos – mounted a successful military coup. The Greek army seized power, civil and political liberties were abolished, and 70 000 political militants were interned on the island of Yaros. A counter-coup failed, and King Constantin II went into exile in Rome that December.

> Just five days after the coup, the Assembly went into action, calling on the Greek authorities to restore the constitutional regime and parliamentary democracy.

A bare five days after the coup, the Assembly went into action, calling on the Greek authorities to restore the constitutional regime and parliamentary democracy, and protesting at their violations of the ECHR. This marked the start of a two-year struggle with the Athens regime, in which the Council of Europe slowly gained the upper hand. The Assembly monitored developments closely and was planning its next move, when Denmark, Norway, Sweden and the Netherlands entered the fray, using the procedure provided for in Article 33 of the ECHR to bring an inter-state application against Greece in the European Court of Human Rights.

THE FIRST CLASH

On 30 January 1969, the Assembly declared *"that the present Greek regime is in serious violation of the conditions for membership of the Council of Europe"*. The path to suspending Greece's membership lay open – the first time that expulsion had ever been used as a threat. The moment of truth came on 12 December 1969, when an Assembly recommendation and a proposal for suspension presented by 11 member states were laid before the Committee of Ministers. After the discussion, but before the vote, the Greek representative announced that his country was withdrawing from the Council, and denounced both the Statute and the ECHR.

The Assembly never lost hope of Greece returning. It watched the evolving situation closely, and kept in touch with leading right-wing and left-wing opponents of the colonels' regime, particularly Constantin Karamanlis and Andreas Papandreou. In January 1974, it listed the conditions which Greece must satisfy to rejoin the Council of Europe, once democracy had been restored. When the colonels were ousted on 23 July 1974, one of the first decisions taken by the new government, under Constantin Karamanlis, was to apply for readmission to the Council.

On 27 September 1974, the Assembly received Evangelos Averoff, Defence Minister and acting Foreign Minister, who, before the coup, had already served for many years as Foreign Minister, and had addressed the Assembly in January 1962, when Greece was chairing the Committee of Ministers. Welcoming him warmly, Assembly President Giuseppe Vedovato declared: *"In spite of the pressure from many sides put on some members of this Assembly to adopt a less intransigent attitude to the military junta in Athens, we reaffirmed our trust in the basic principles of democracy and respect for human rights, and our determination has never faltered. Today, in this chamber, we know we were right and that, in spite of the attitude adopted by some in the name of political realism, we must not stray from the path laid down for us by the Council of Europe's Statute. Our*

The Mediterranean dimension

■ **Evangelos Averoff, Greek Foreign Minister and Chairman-in-Office of the Committee of Ministers (centre), and Georg Kahn-Ackermann, Secretary General of the Council of Europe (right),** *Strasbourg,* 1976.

Parliamentary Assembly is still inspired by that same spirit, for it is and must remain the faithful guardian of the principles on which our parliamentary democracies are based."

Evangelos Averoff began his speech by declaring that he had come to the Assembly *"to announce the end of a dictatorship and the rebirth of a democracy"*. He detailed the measures taken by the new democratic government, which had been sworn in on 24 July 1975: release of all political prisoners and a general amnesty for political offences; enforced retirement of some 40 generals and renewed political control of the army; repeal of the colonels' decrees on trade unionism, and drafting of new laws; restoration of the democratic constitution of 1952; passing of a law permitting political parties to exist and operate, subject only to their promising not to attempt to overthrow the democratic regime; legalisation of the Greek Communist Party, which had been banned since 1947. He announced that a new electoral law had been passed, and that elections would be held in the first half of November. These elections were duly held on 17 November 1974, and an Assembly delegation went to Greece for the occasion. On 28 November, Greece rejoined the Council of Europe.

CYPRUS – FROM INDEPENDENCE TO COUNCIL OF EUROPE MEMBERSHIP

Cyprus first appeared on the Assembly's agenda in 1952, long before it became independent, in August 1960.

Minister Averoff started by declaring that he had come "to announce the end of a dictatorship and the rebirth of a democracy".

The Mediterranean dimension

In 1955, the UN General Assembly rejected Greece's request for a debate on Cyprus.

In 1955, Greece tried – unsuccessfully – to raise the Cyprus problem in the UN General Assembly. A number of Greek parliamentarians then brought the matter up in the Strasbourg Assembly and proposed the setting up of a special committee to tackle it. The Assembly responded by offering to help the governments concerned to find a solution.

In October 1958, the Assembly discussed a general report on the policies of Council of Europe member states. Seven foreign ministers or secretaries of state attended, including the Turkish and United Kingdom ministers. Attention focused on the UK government's plan for Cyprus, and on the proposal put forward by Archbishop Makarios that the island be made independent, with UN guarantees to protect the rights of the Turkish minority.

In February 1959, the United Kingdom, Greece and Turkey concluded the Zurich and London agreements on independence for Cyprus.

The island became independent in 1960, and applied for Council of Europe membership in March 1961. On 24 April, the Assembly noted that the Cypriot Constitution embodied the human rights guarantees required by the ECHR, and told the Committee of Ministers that it approved its admission. A Cypriot delegation, representing both the island's communities and led by Glafcos Clerides, future president of the Republic of Cyprus, came to Strasbourg for the September 1961 session.

THE PROBLEM OF REPRESENTATION IN THE ASSEMBLY

The delegation had three full members – two Greek Cypriots and one Turkish Cypriot – and as many substitutes. Early in 1964, however, a serious institutional crisis was sparked by tensions within the government, and the Turkish Cypriot ministers staged a walk-out. The composition of the Cypriot delegation at once became an issue in the Assembly.

In April, the Assembly refused to ratify the credentials of a delegation consisting solely of Greek Cypriots, and insisted that there must be a full member and a substitute drawn from the Turkish Cypriot community. No agreement could be reached and, for the next 19 years, Cyprus was not represented in the Assembly. Finally, in May 1983, the Assembly put an end to this situation by agreeing to admit a mini-delegation – the President of the Cypriot parliament, plus a substitute.

In 1995, the Assembly pointed out that the Turkish Cypriot community still lacked a voice at the Council of Europe. It decided to remedy this by inviting political representatives of both communities to all committee meetings at which matters directly relevant to Cyprus were discussed – and confirmed this decision in Resolution 1113 (1997).

In 2002, it decided *"to explore ways to integrate more closely the elected representatives of the Turkish Cypriot community in the work of the Parliamentary Assembly and its committees, beyond the framework of Assembly Resolution 1113 (1997), and integrated to the Cypriot delegation"*.

■ **Glafcos Clerides, President of the Republic of Cyprus,**
in the Assembly Chamber,
12 April 1994.

When the Kofi Annan plan was rejected in the April 2004 referendum, the Assembly declared that it was *"unfair for the Turkish Cypriot community, which has expressed clear support for a reunited and European Cyprus, to continue to be denied representation in the European political debate"*. It confirmed its decision of 2002 and instructed the Bureau to devise ways of giving it effect.

The Assembly refused to admit a delegation with only Greek Cypriot members and insisted that the Turkish Cypriot community must also be represented.

Finally, on 4 October 2004, it invited two elected representatives of the Turkish Cypriot community to attend its sessions, with the right to speak, but not to vote.

DIVIDED ISLAND

When army officers close to the Greek junta staged a coup on the island, Turkey landed troops on 20 July 1974, basing this move on Article 4 of the Treaty of Guarantee of 16 August 1960 (signed by Cyprus, Greece, Turkey and the UK). The completed operation left 40% of the island in Turkish hands.

The Assembly immediately called a meeting of the Standing Committee to discuss the situation. The Political Affairs Committee's rapporteur on this occasion was Franz Karasek, a future Secretary General of the Council of Europe.

The Assembly condemned the coup, called for dialogue between the two communities, and offered to help broker a political settlement. It also set up a special working party, consisting of the

Political Affairs Committee's rapporteur and the chairmen of the political groups, to investigate the situation and report on it.

It again discussed Cyprus in 1976 and insisted, in Resolution 615 (1976), that there must be a settlement which guaranteed the sovereignty of a united and independent Republic of Cyprus, and maintained its territorial integrity. Concerning the structure of the Cypriot state, it appealed to the island's two communities to resume direct negotiations and work out a formula for political co-existence.

In November 1983, the northern part of the island proclaimed itself independent, and was recognised as such by Turkey. After a further debate on 23 November, the Assembly urged the Turkish Cypriot leaders to reverse their decision, deplored the unilateral act of recognition whereby one member state – Turkey – had approved division of another, and called for immediate withdrawal of the Turkish occupying forces. In Recommendation 974 (1983), it urged the Committee of Ministers to *"reject decisively the unilateral declaration of independence proclaimed in the north of Cyprus"*, and asked it to mediate between the two communities. It also suggested that the chairman of the committee should remain in close, ongoing contact with the Secretary General of the United Nations, and make it clear that the Council of Europe was ready to take or support any action which seemed likely to promote the resumption of productive dialogue between the two Cypriot communities.

The Assembly condemned the coup, called for dialogue between the two communities, and offered to help find a political solution.

The Mediterranean dimension

On 24 November 1983, the Committee of Ministers adopted Resolution (83) 13 in which it denounced the declaration of independence as *"legally invalid"* and called for its withdrawal.

In July 1990, the Republic of Cyprus applied for EU membership for the whole island. The positive opinion on the application adopted by the European Commission in June 1993 encouraged the Assembly to take further initiatives from 1995 on.

TURKEY — THE ARMY TAKES OVER

Turkey's democratic stability has been imperilled more than once in the course of its long Council of Europe membership, and the Assembly has always been there to help when needed. Prime Minister Bülent Ecevit acknowledged this plainly when he addressed it on 10 May 1979: *"When the ebb of economic and social forces has tried to pull us away from the course of democracy, our membership in the Council of Europe has served as a compass, helping to hold us to that course. Democracy's main safeguard – in Turkey, as in any other country – is inevitably the people's attachment to democracy and freedom, but there have been times when our Council membership has helped to prevent us from losing our bearings."*

On 12 September 1980, the army, led by General Kenan Evren, declared that the country was in "mortal danger", and used this as a pretext to seize power, dissolve the democratic political institutions established by the 1961 Constitution, and install a National Security Council, with both legislative and executive powers, in their stead.

On 23 November, the Assembly deplored the fact that one member state had unilaterally approved division of another.

Without formally denouncing the ECHR, the new regime used Article 15 of that text to evade it. This provides that states may provisionally, *"in time of war or other public emergency threatening the life of the nation"*, disregard some of their obligations. The military, of course, ignored the fact that certain core obligations may never be waived, and that the right to life, the prohibition on torture, and the ban on retroactive law-making are absolute.

NEXT STEP, PARLIAMENTARY SANCTIONS

The new Turkish leaders were desperate to avoid breaking with the Council of Europe. On 2 April 1981, the Turkish Permanent Representative assured the Assembly's Political Affairs Committee that his government attached special importance to membership of – and co-operation with – the Council.

Although parliament had been dissolved, the military regime actually offered to make special arrangements, so that former parliamentarians, who were members of the Assembly, could continue to attend its sessions – and were even planning to renew the old delegation's mandate for the May 1981 session.

At the Assembly's request, its President, Hans J. de Koster, went to Ankara and Istanbul (12-15 April 1981), to seek more information on the Turkish authorities' timetable for a phased return to democracy, and assurances on other matters of concern to the Assembly. He talked to members of the National Security Council and government (including General Evren), former MPs,

The Mediterranean dimension

"When the ebb of economic and social forces has tried to pull us away from the course of democracy, our membership in the Council of Europe has served as a compass, helping to hold us to that course. Democracy's main safeguard — in Turkey, as in any other country — is inevitably the people's attachment to democracy and freedom, but there have been times when our Council membership has helped to prevent us from losing our bearings."

Bülent Ecevit, Prime Minister of Turkey, *addressing the Assembly, 10 May 1979.*

members of the Turkish delegation to the Assembly, and some former political leaders. The member states' diplomatic representatives in Turkey also gave him their impressions, helping to fill in the picture.

Subjects covered included the human rights situation, prospects for a return to democracy, relations between Turkey and the Council of Europe, Turkish representation in the Assembly, and the fate of members of the Turkish delegation who had been arrested. The President presented his conclusions at the Assembly's May 1981 session.

In an exhaustive report on Turkey's problems, he declared: *"The 'countdown' for the return to parliamentary democracy will begin in June 1981 with the announcement of the modalities for setting up the Constituent Assembly. This is to be followed by the announcement in the autumn of 1981 of the timing of the elections, which are to take place in the autumn of 1982 or the spring of 1983, the choice depending on the termination of the Constituent Assembly's work on the draft constitution. […] Most of my interlocutors, including Mr Ecevit, felt that it would be inappropriate to exercise pressure for advancing the proposed timing of the election. […] Nevertheless, in view of its Statute, it is clear that the Council of Europe must follow very carefully developments between now and the establishment of a new parliament and make its voice heard, whenever necessary, to ensure respect for human rights and fundamental freedoms, and preclude erosion of the substance of democracy before the formal return to democratic institutions."*

A break with Strasbourg was the last thing the new regime wanted.

Parliament had been dissolved, but the military suggested special arrangements, so that former MPs could keep coming to Strasbourg.

Responding to suggestions on sanctions, he said: *"So far, the present government has not acted against the interests of the vast majority of the Turkish people. For this reason, and in the light of the assurances given, it is my personal belief that no action under Article 8 of the Statute is called for at this moment."*

Referring to Turkish representation in the Assembly, he saw *"a number of practical advantages in following the majority view of the Committee on Rules of Procedure that the present Turkish delegation should be prolonged for the duration of the 33rd session"* (May 1981 to May 1982).

However, on 14 May 1981, the Assembly decided that the previous autumn's coup left it no choice but to suspend the Turkish delegation, declaring that *"it would be out of order to envisage the prolongation of the term of office of the Turkish parliamentary delegation to the Council of Europe"* and that it looked forward to the time when developments in Turkey would allow it to *"welcome back in its midst an elected and properly constituted Turkish delegation"*.

For that, it had to wait until January 1984 – but the Turkish question remained on its agenda in the meantime. At one point, it even considered asking the Committee of Ministers to apply the sanctions covered by the Statute, and expel Turkey, but a majority of the members thought that keeping it in would allow the Council of Europe to step up the pressure and offer better hopes of securing a return to democracy.

In June 1982, Denmark, France, the Netherlands, Norway and Sweden decided to bring an inter-state case against Turkey before the European Court of Human Rights under Article 33 of the ECHR. However, a friendly settlement was secured, and a detailed timetable agreed for the restoration of democracy.

The Motherland Party triumphed in the parliamentary elections held on 6 November 1983, and the junta stepped down, opening the way for a Turkish delegation's return to the Assembly in January 1984. At first, its credentials were contested under Resolution 803 (1983), but the Assembly approved them in May, feeling that this would hasten adoption of the measures essential to the establishment of a true democracy and genuine respect for human rights in Turkey.

After that, relations between Turkey and the Council of Europe came back to normal. In 1986, the Assembly's summer meetings (Standing Committee, Bureau, several specialised committees and Joint Committee) were held in Istanbul, and Turkey took over the chair of the Committee of Ministers in November that year.

This was the context in which Vahit Halefoğlu, Turkish Minister for Foreign Affairs, addressed the Assembly on 28 January 1987. Having presented the Committee of Ministers' official communication as its Chairman, he then made a statement as minister on Turkey's relations with the Council. Among other things, he said: *"Turkey's decision to join the Council of Europe was a natural consequence of her attachment to common values and aspirations, such as devotion to parliamentary democracy, based on the rule of law and respect for human rights, which constitute the*

On 14 May 1981, the Assembly decided that the situation created by the coup left it no choice – and suspended the Turkish delegation.

> The Motherland Party's victory in the elections on 6 November 1983 led to the junta's stepping down.

basic pillars of the Organisation. We experienced some difficulties in our relations with the Council after 1980, owing to the temporary suspension of the parliamentary system. However, we maintained our dialogue with the Organisation throughout that difficult transitional period. The Turkish people's determination to uphold the democratic parliamentary system, and their firm belief in the virtues of a society based on human rights and fundamental freedoms, certainly helped to keep that dialogue going. The Turkish parliamentarians' return to the Parliamentary Assembly in 1984 placed it on a wider and more fruitful basis. In other words, the Turkish parliamentarians have contributed greatly to a better understanding by this august body of the evolving situation in Turkey." He also announced that the Turkish Council of Ministers had decided to recognise the authority of the European Commission of Human Rights to consider applications brought by individuals, non-governmental organisations or groups of individuals, under Article 25 of the ECHR.

However, democratic stability and human rights were still not fully guaranteed, and the Assembly instructed its Political and Legal Affairs Committees to watch the situation closely. When a further debate on Turkey was held in June 1992, the Assembly noted – in spite of real progress since 1984 and of the government's good intentions – that human rights were still being violated. In Resolution 985 (1992), it put forward a comprehensive list of the constitutional and legislative reforms needed to right the situation. There were fresh problems when several leaders of the Democracy Party (DEP) were arrested for supporting the Kurdish cause in March 1994, and the party itself was banned in June.

The Assembly took the matter up. After a debate in plenary session, it instructed the Bureau to send its President, Miguel Ángel Martínez (Spain), to Ankara with a delegation, to make on-the-spot enquiries and talk to the Turkish authorities. The delegation went to Turkey in September 1994, and was asked to: pinpoint constitutional and legislative reforms which were needed to bring the Turkish legal system into line with European values (as requested by the Assembly in June 1992), investigate practices which violated human rights and democratic freedoms, and discuss the Kurdish question and the situation in the south-eastern provinces with the Turkish authorities. It talked to MPs and members of the government, including the Prime Minister, Mrs Tansu Çiller. President Martínez reported back to the Assembly on 3 October 1994. He said that discussions had been frank and open, and that the Turkish authorities had promised to carry out the reforms asked for by the Assembly, and had given the delegation a timetable for this. The mission had been a successful example of parliamentary diplomacy, and had shown how useful an on-the-spot Assembly presence could be at times of political conflict or crisis. He hoped that there would be more such missions in the future. The Assembly instructed its Political and Legal Affairs Committees to monitor Turkey's implementation of the undertakings it had given.

The Turkish Foreign Minister announced that his country had decided to recognise the authority of the European Commission of Human Rights.

MALTA COMES ON BOARD

In December 1964, the UK and Italian delegations notified the Committee of Ministers that Malta wished to join the Council of

Europe. Consulted, the Assembly broke new ground by referring the application to one of its committees – the Political Affairs Committee. This gave it an opportunity to lay down certain principles concerning its role in the accession process, and it scored another first by indicating that Malta should sign and ratify the ECHR as soon as possible after joining.

MALTESE PROPOSALS

The Maltese Prime Minister, Giorgio Borg Olivier, spoke in the Assembly twice – on 4 May 1964, when Malta joined the Council, and again on 3 May 1969, when the Council of Europe celebrated its 20th anniversary.

He suggested that the Council of Europe might find two aspects of Malta's foreign policy – its emphasis on the Mediterranean and North Africa, and its determination to promote co-operation and détente in Europe, regardless of the East/West divide – useful, and urged it to become active in both these areas.

Malta's first turn to chair the Committee of Ministers came in 1978, and Prime Minister Dom Mintoff addressed the Assembly in September. Having first spoken for the Committee as its Chairman, he struck a personal note in his comments on the situation in Europe and the world at large.

In his view, western Europe had missed the opportunities offered by the success of the *Ostpolitik*, which – in spite of temporary setbacks – had achieved real détente in Europe. It had also failed

In June 1992, the Assembly noted that – in spite of progress made since 1984 and the government's good intentions – human rights were still being violated in Turkey.

to move towards becoming a third force and asserting its independence on the international scene, while maintaining its economic and cultural ties with the two superpowers.

He regretted the Council of Europe's failure to respond when repeatedly urged by Malta to make thorough preparations for two meetings under the auspices of the Conference on Security and Co-operation in Europe (CSCE) – one in Malta on economic, scientific and cultural co-operation in the Mediterranean (1979), the other in Madrid on Mediterranean security (1980).

CREDENTIALS CRISIS

On 24 April 1980, the President of the Maltese Parliament notified the President of the Assembly that the Maltese delegation's mandate was being suspended with immediate effect, since the opposition had broken the agreement on "pairing", officially valid for the life of parliament.

The crisis lasted until the mid-1980s. In September 1985, the Maltese Parliament despatched a one-man delegation (the man being its President) to Strasbourg. This solution failed to impress the Assembly, which refused to approve the credentials submitted and referred the whole matter to the Committee on Rules of Procedure and Immunities. The latter proposed postponing discussion of its report to the January 1986 part-session – but by then a full Maltese delegation, including opposition members, had been appointed, and the Assembly accepted its credentials.

The Mediterranean dimension

■ **Malta joins the Council of Europe,**
Left to right: Peter Smithers, Secretary General of the Council of Europe, Giorgio Borg Olivier, Prime Minister of Malta, Pierre Pflimlin, President of the Assembly, and Polys Modinos, Deputy Secretary General of the Council of Europe, before the Palais de l'Europe,
4 May 1965.

The whole incident strengthened the Assembly's determination to insist that parliamentary delegations must genuinely reflect their home political spectrum. In November 1989, it added a new rule to its Rules of Procedure, making it possible to contest the credentials of any delegation whose membership failed to reflect its parliament's make-up.

In general, co-operation between Malta and the Council of Europe is marked by the fact that many Maltese politicians have served in the Assembly and have gained their experience of European parliamentary life in Strasbourg. The list has included presidents (Antony Buttigieg, Vincent Tabone, Guido de Marco), prime ministers (Dominic Mintoff, Michael Gonzi, Guze Cassar), foreign ministers (Alex Sceberras Trigona, John Vella) and presidents of parliament (Daniel Micallef, Francis Agius, Paul Xuereb).

PORTUGAL'S PATH TO THE COUNCIL OF EUROPE

From 1951 on, relations with Portugal and Spain were one of the concerns of the Special Committee on European nations not represented in the Council (later the Committee on Relations with European Non-Member Countries), which suggested that their ability to accept all or part of the ECHR – an essential condition for joining the Council of Europe – should be investigated. It was also thought that they might be allowed to accede to the European Cultural Convention and some of the Council's social conventions.

Malta chaired the Committee of Ministers for the first time in 1978.

In 1970, the Committee on Relations with European Non-Member Countries decided to produce a report on the situation in Portugal. Preparing it involved contacting various leaders of the anti-Salazar movement (including Mário Soares), and this caused a considerable stir in Portugal itself.

> The Maltese incident left the Assembly determined to insist that delegations must reflect their home parliament's make-up.

The Committee invited Mário Soares to attend when it discussed the report in Strasbourg on 17 April, during the Assembly's session. He was also present in the Chamber when the Assembly itself discussed it in plenary session on 20 April – and this was one of the factors which led the Caetano government to exile him.

Portugal's relations with the Council of Europe took off rapidly after the Carnation Revolution of 25 April 1974. Within two weeks, the Assembly was publicly welcoming the fall of the dictatorship and the new regime's determination to bring back democracy and terminate the colonial wars (it insisted that the future of Portugal's colonial possessions must be decided with reference to the principles of self-determination and decolonisation laid down by the UN). It also showed its faith in the country's democratic future by declaring that it hoped to see it join the Council soon. In fact, although the dictatorship had gone, Portugal's institutions still fell short of European standards, and stability had yet to be attained. Indeed, the Communists tried to seize power on 28 September 1974. Mário Soares, now Foreign Minister, had just arrived in Strasbourg from the UN General Assembly in New York and was preparing to address the Assembly. He gave it a blow-by-blow account of events, based on information received just before, and during, the sitting. Referring to the Carnation Revolution, he declared: *"The resolve to replace the dictatorship overthrown on 25 April by a democratic regime was demonstrated unmistakably by the close union between the Armed Forces Movement, the parties and the democratic forces of the Portuguese people – a circumstance which confers an uncontested de facto legitimacy on the provisional constitutional regime at present in force in Portugal."* He addressed a ringing appeal to the Assembly: *"The Portuguese Government believes it should be able to become a member of the Council of Europe as soon as free elections for a constituent assembly have been held. These elections will, in fact, constitute not only the basic criterion for the expression of a multi-party democracy but, from the point of view of the general theory of political rights, the constituent assembly then elected must be regarded as the highest expression of the sovereign power of the people. Pending the achievement of these aims, my government hopes to be able to obtain for Portugal observer status with the Council of Europe."* His eloquence was not lost on the Assembly, which turned at once to the practical question of helping Portugal to find speedy solutions to the pressing political, social and administrative problems which stood between it and progressive installation of a democratic system. Its answer was the "special fund for co-operation with Portugal" – the first post-accession assistance programme for a new member.

Promulgation of the constitution in May 1976, the holding of free and fair elections to the Constituent Assembly and the Assembly of the Republic, the election of a president, and a vote of confidence in the new government were decisive stages on Portugal's

From 1951 on, relations with Portugal and Spain were on the agenda of the Special Committee on European nations not represented in the Council.

Two weeks after the Carnation Revolution, the Assembly hailed the fall of the dictatorship in Portugal.

path to Council of Europe membership. The Assembly also welcomed the armed forces' decision to acknowledge the supremacy of the elected civil authorities, retaining only the role of adviser and guarantor. It asked for, and received, assurances concerning certain sections of the constitution which seemed hard to square with democratic and human rights principles, for example the preamble and Article 1, which called for a transition to Socialism and the democratic taking of power by the working class, and Article 82.2, which established a Revolutionary Council, manned by members of the armed forces.

The Assembly's support for the young democracy was made plain on 16 September 1976, when it adopted a favourable opinion on Portugal's joining the Council of Europe – which it did on 22 September.

Just over a year later, on 28 September 1977, Mário Soares again addressed the Assembly – this time as his country's Prime Minister. He spoke with deep emotion of his first visit, in September 1974, and declared: *"We continue to hope that European collaboration and solidarity, of which the Council of Europe is irrefutable evidence, will help us win through, not only so that Portugal can remain the free and democratic country it has chosen to be, but also in order to strengthen democratic principles in Europe, as well as those spiritual and moral values which, as is stated in the Preamble to the Council of Europe's Statute, constitute the common heritage of the European peoples represented here. Today more than ever, most Europeans are aware, firstly, of the inestimable benefits of democracy and,*

The Mediterranean dimension

■ **Mário Soares, Portuguese Foreign Minister,** *addressing the Assembly,* 28 September 1974.

"The Portuguese Government believes it should be able to become a member of the Council of Europe as soon as free elections for a constituent assembly have been held."

secondly, of the grave dangers which threaten it. Today more than ever, the Europe represented in this Council – far though it may be from political unification – recognises the interdependence of its constituent parts. Democracy and freedom are indivisible. Every citizen, every government, every country which supports Portuguese democracy is thereby supporting its own democracy."

SPAIN

Way back in 1950, the Assembly had already expressed the hope that Spanish parliamentarians might soon be able to attend its sessions – and Spain was not forgotten by its Special Committee on European nations not represented in the Council.

At the time, many people felt that the strong line taken by Spain and Portugal in defending Europe's freedom and security against any threat from the Eastern bloc made them suitable for Council of Europe membership. However, there were principles and values which the Assembly prized more than security.

In fact, from 1955 on, Spain did participate in some of the Council of Europe's intergovernmental activities. It acceded to the European Cultural Convention on 4 July 1957, and this allowed it to take part – on the same footing as members – in cultural activities (in the Council's very broad meaning of that term), to which it also contributed financially.

In December 1960, the Special Committee on European nations not represented in the Council had talks in Paris with Salvador de Madariaga and two other Spanish representatives. It also tackled the thorny issue of an amnesty for political prisoners in Spain.

In 1962, Spain sought to open negotiations with the European Economic Community (EEC) on some form of association. Reports submitted to the Assembly that year by the Economic Affairs Committee also urged EEC governments to explore the possibility of concluding some form of economic agreement between Spain and the EEC. The Assembly insisted, however, that certain changes would be needed in the Spanish Constitution before any political links could be considered.

In the second half of the 1960s, Spain made various efforts to enhance its presence at the Council of Europe. In 1967, it established a special mission in Strasbourg. In 1970, it applied for observer status with the Council. The Committee of Ministers decided to uphold the practice which allowed non-member states to appoint observers to its subsidiary bodies.

Between 1974 and 1977, the Assembly watched closely as the Franco era drew to an end, and democracy was gradually introduced. It discussed the situation in Spain on no less than six occasions during that period – and always in terms which favoured Spanish accession.

The Assembly did, however, name its conditions: human rights must be restored, political prisoners and exiles must be amnestied,

A favourable opinion on Portugal's joining the Council of Europe, adopted on 16 September 1976, showed that the young democracy had the Assembly's backing. It became a member on 22 September.

> In 1950, the Assembly was already expressing the hope that Spanish parliamentarians might soon be able to attend its sessions.

and political parties and trade unions must be allowed to play a full part in giving the country democratic structures.

In September 1976, the Assembly noted that the democratic process in Spain was now irreversible. It welcomed the amnesty granted by the King to political prisoners and exiles. It also stressed the importance of press and media freedom, political and trade union liberties, and legalisation of all the country's political parties.

Ten months later, in July 1977, the Assembly paid tribute to the maturity shown by the Spanish people in voting for democratic parties in elections to the Cortès. It expressed the hope that the process now under way would rapidly produce a full democracy, in which human rights were guaranteed.

In October 1977, a high-level Cortès delegation, including Fernando Álvarez de Miranda, Felipe González and Santiago Carrillo, was invited to Strasbourg by the President of the Assembly. The members of the latter were well aware that Spain's young democracy was still imperfect, and that a new constitution was merely at the drafting stage – but their last reservations were banished by the impassioned eloquence with which their guests argued the case for Spain's joining the Council of Europe. An important part in tipping the scale was played by the speech delivered by Marcelino Oreja, Spanish Foreign Minister and later Secretary General of the Council of Europe, and a joint undertaking by all the parties in the Cortès that the rule of law and the ideals enshrined in the ECHR would be fully guaranteed in the new constitution. In a unanimous final vote, the Assembly affirmed its confidence in the Spanish democratic process.

On 8 October 1979, His Majesty Juan Carlos I, King of Spain, declared in the Assembly: *"In addressing this Assembly I cannot forget the crucial part it played in Spain's accession to the Council of Europe, causing it to depart in some ways from custom, in both form and timing, so that its faith and hope in the transition to democracy in Spain might prevail. For it was this Assembly which, with an impatience which we Spaniards greatly appreciated, was the first to put its full trust in the legitimate representatives of the Spanish people, as soon as it gained control of its destiny. But, to go beyond the specific case of my country, I should like to pay tribute here to this Assembly for its essential contribution both to the realisation of the concept of European unity and to the furtherance of values which are an inherent part of our civilisation, particularly the freedom, dignity and fundamental rights of the individual, which form the basis for political stability and social peace. From 1949 to 1979, no significant event occurred, nor did any way open offering cause for hope, without this Assembly making a real contribution, or ensuring it of a resounding impact, if indeed it had not already taken the initiative itself."*

The King of Spain addressed the Assembly again on 26 January 1988, as Honorary President of the European Public Campaign for North-South Interdependence and Solidarity, launched in Madrid in November 1987.

The Mediterranean dimension

■ **His Majesty Juan Carlos I, King of Spain (right), with Assembly President Hans J. de Koster,** 8 October 1979.

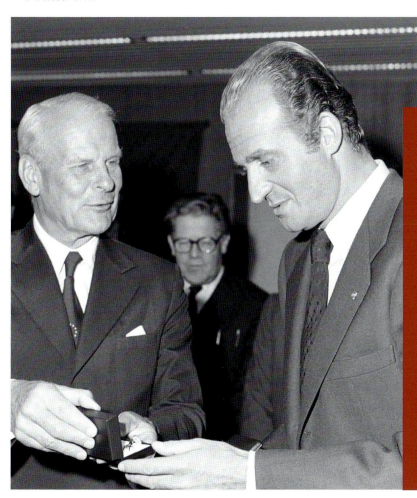

"In addressing this Assembly I cannot forget the crucial part it played in Spain's accession to the Council of Europe, causing it to depart in some ways from custom, in both form and timing, so that its faith and hope in the transition to democracy in Spain might prevail. For it was this Assembly which, with an impatience which we Spaniards greatly appreciated, was the first to put its full trust in the legitimate representatives of the Spanish people, as soon as it gained control of its destiny."

Relations with the Israeli Parliament (Knesset)

Relations with the Knesset were initiated when the Standing Committee decided, on 5 July 1957, to invite a parliamentary delegation from Israel to attend that year's October session on an ad hoc basis. This invitation was subsequently renewed.

In Resolution 195 (1961), the Assembly introduced observer status, making it possible to admit as observers official representatives of non-member states, appointed with their parliaments' approval, who were allowed to sit in the Assembly, but not to speak (unless authorised to do so by the Bureau), and also to attend committee meetings on certain conditions.

The Israeli delegation was immediately awarded this status and, ever since, Knesset representatives have been regulars at Assembly sessions and meetings of Assembly committees, as well as taking part in other activities, for example the Strasbourg Conferences on Parliamentary Democracy and the Conferences of Presidents and Speakers of European Parliaments. Several Assembly committees have also held meetings in Israel.

The developing dialogue with the Knesset prompted the Assembly to invite various Israeli leaders to Strasbourg. One was Prime Minister Golda Meir, who addressed it on 1 October 1973. Praising Europe's approach to reconciliation, she declared: *"Maybe it is a dream to hope that the time will come when our area will duplicate what Europe has done. But many dreams of ours have come true. Anyway, only to the extent that they have the courage to dream do individuals or countries have the courage also to execute their hopes and dreams. We dream and we hope that the time will come when our area will duplicate what Europe has done, that together we shall discuss problems, and, what is even more important, that together we shall build our area in real co-operation, knowing that not one single people in our area can be happier if any other people is destroyed. The happiness of all the people in the entire area depends upon our all living there in peace and in co-operation."*

Other prominent Israeli visitors have included Foreign Ministers Abba Eban and Moshe Dayan, and Prime Ministers Shimon Peres (1986) and Yitzhak Rabin (1994), as well as the President of Israel, Chaim Herzog (1992).

The Assembly's links with Israel also led it to take a closer interest in the Middle East conflict. In 1979, the Political Affairs Committee set up a Sub-Committee on the Middle East, which strove to initiate dialogue between Palestinian representatives and Israeli parliamentarians.

With the passing of time, the Assembly's commitment to working for peace in that region increased, and it stepped up its efforts from the 1990s on.

The Assembly – source of ideas, beacon of democracy

"It is the duty of the Council of Europe to contribute at the same time towards the unification of a free and democratic Europe and the easing of tension which has begun between the East and the West."

■ **Recommendation 389 (1964).**

The Assembly – source of ideas, beacon of democracy

In the early 1960s, the Assembly realised that its hopes of seeing the Council of Europe entrusted with the task of co-ordinating the principal aspects of the European project were doomed to disappointment, and that the future integrated Europe would be based on the European Communities, established by the Paris (1951) and Rome (1957) treaties. The EEC held its first European Summit in Paris in February 1961. In November of that year, France put forward the Fouchet Plan for voluntary political union, and several new countries applied to join the EEC. However, France's veto on the UK joining blocked expansion, and the EEC's membership stayed limited to six until 1 January 1973.

These developments convinced the Assembly that – alongside the Brussels/Luxembourg Communities, with their still limited powers and far smaller membership – the Council of Europe should press ahead with its task of rallying as many European states as possible around the key principles of human rights, the rule of law and pluralist democracy.

In fact, the Council of Europe was still trying to find its role, although the European Court of Human Rights, which was established in 1959 and gave its first judgment in 1961, had gone some way towards giving it a fresh impetus.

In May 1963, the Assembly elected Pierre Pflimlin, French MP and Mayor of Strasbourg, as its President. A year later, it elected Peter Smithers, UK Under-Secretary of State for Foreign Affairs, Secretary General of the Council of Europe.

The Council of Europe was seeking a role. The European Court of Human Rights, which was established in 1959 and gave its first judgment in 1961, helped to give it a fresh impetus.

All of these were positive developments, and the Assembly took them as a basis for forging ahead. It played a very active part in enlargement of the Council of Europe, which – following the accession of Cyprus (1961), Switzerland (1963), Malta (1965), Portugal (1976), Spain (1977) and Liechtenstein (1978) – had 21 members by the end of the 1970s.

Between 1960 and 1980, the Assembly pressed resolutely ahead with its standard-setting work – an activity which effectively made it Europe's ethical and democratic conscience. At the same time, its policy of inviting prominent statesmen to address it turned it into a major political forum for leaders from Europe and outside, who came to Strasbourg to expound their plans and voice their anxieties. Finally, it initiated contacts with the countries of eastern Europe, and organised debates on the Conference on Security and Co-operation in Europe (CSCE), thus giving it the parliamentary and democratic dimension which it otherwise lacked.

EUROPEAN LAW – THE ASSEMBLY'S CONTRIBUTION

Many people are unaware that, in the early 1960s – well before the European Community – the Council of Europe led the way in harmonising European law on a wide range of technical issues, for example patents, recognition of diplomas, social and medical assistance, simplified frontier formalities, compulsory motor insurance, suspension of driving licences and punishment of road traffic offences. Its sensitivity to social change allowed it to extend its work to social, cultural and environmental issues, and its ability to

The Assembly's invitations policy made it a major political forum for statesmen from Europe and outside, who used it to voice their visions and anxieties.

foresee future problems was reflected in its pioneering work on the new threats to democracy and human rights posed by terrorism.

Fighting terrorism

The Assembly first tackled terrorism in its work on air piracy in the late 1960s. At that time, it saw increased co-operation between governments at world level as the best hope of a solution. In 1972, after the tragedy at the Munich Olympics, where 11 Israeli athletes died in a savage terrorist attack, it called for European action. In Recommendation 684 (1972) on international terrorism, it noted that *"such acts, which are in utter conflict with the traditions and practices governing international relations, raise, in entirely new terms, the question of the responsibility of governments to put an end to them"*, and asked the Committee of Ministers to *"work out, in close co-operation, a joint European front to combat terrorism, and to make this a permanent item on its agenda as from its 51st session in December 1972"*, and also to *"invite the governments of member states to use all their political and economic influence"* to deter certain states from harbouring terrorists while they planned their crimes, and granting them asylum afterwards.

In Recommendation 703 (1973), it urged member governments to adopt an agreed definition of terrorism, making it impossible to plead "political" justification for acts which endangered the lives of innocent people. It asked the Committee of Ministers to convene without delay a special conference, at which ministers of the interior, or other ministers responsible for police and home security in Council of Europe member states, could work out joint

> The Assembly first tackled terrorism in its work on air piracy in the late 1960s.

proposals and co-ordinate measures aimed at preventing acts of terrorism. The upshot was a conference of European ministers of justice, which was held in Obernai (near Strasbourg) in May 1975, and contributed very usefully to further work on this question.

By working hand in hand with governments, the Assembly realised its aim of formulating Europe's first anti-terrorist norms at the Council of Europe. These were embodied in the 1977 European Convention on the Suppression of Terrorism, which – in spite of certain flaws – has the merit of providing clearly for the extradition or prosecution of terrorists. The Assembly's awareness of the terrible threat to democracy and law inherent in terrorism kept it working on the question, gradually refining its views and proposals. In Recommendation 852 (1979), it looked at the causes of terrorism and tackled the problem of media coverage of terrorist acts. It also insisted that anti-terrorist measures – although vital to preserve democratic institutions – must themselves respect the values enshrined in those institutions, national constitutions and the ECHR.

It proposed using the Council of Europe's intergovernmental machinery to promote co-operation between courts, police and intelligence services in the member states. It also urged governments to start work on establishing a common legal area, covering all the Council's member states.

In November 1980, the Assembly organised the first major international conference on defending democracy against terrorism, with Franco Calamandrei of the Italian Senate as rapporteur. Its Recommendation 916 (1981), adopted in the wake of that

Thanks to the Assembly, Europe's first anti-terrorist norms were formulated at the Council of Europe, and embodied in the 1977 European Convention on the Suppression of Terrorism.

The Assembly – source of ideas, beacon of democracy

In 1986, the Assembly proposed that the member states define terrorism as a crime against humanity.

conference, covered two new aspects of the question, asking the Committee of Ministers to promote a uniform definition of terrorism in both national and international law, and also to commission an intergovernmental study of the role of culture, education and the media in preventing and suppressing terrorism.

In a 1986 resolution, it took an even harder line on terrorism, suggesting that the member states define it as a crime against humanity. It kept this issue on its agenda, later proposing that a definition of terrorism be added to the 1977 convention.

A global convention on preventing and suppressing terrorism was another, subsequent proposal, and its efforts to secure this were crowned with success in 2005.

Working together against crime – treating prison inmates humanely

In the early 1950s, with crime going international, the Assembly was already insisting on the need for a European convention on extradition – and this was adopted and opened for signing in 1957. Another brainchild was the European Convention on the Transfer of Proceedings in Criminal Matters, opened for signing in 1972. Taken together, these texts – with the European Convention on Mutual Assistance in Criminal Matters (1959) and the European Convention on the International Validity of Criminal Judgments (1970) – virtually amounted to a European code for mutual aid in criminal proceedings, making life easier for national authorities, and paving the way for more sweeping action by the European Community in the 1980s.

Ensuring that prison inmates were treated humanely was another Assembly concern. It helped to draft minimum rules on this question in the 1970s, and revise them in 1987, and later proposed preparation of a European Prison Charter.

Children's rights

The Assembly produced several reports on children's rights from 1958 on, and its Recommendation 292 (1961) directly inspired the European Convention on the Adoption of Children (1967). It was also involved in preparing the European Convention on the Legal Status of Children Born out of Wedlock, which was opened for signing in 1975. It later worked on the legal situation and rights of children, maltreatment of children, and exploitation of children for purposes of prostitution, child pornography and child labour.

Transfrontier co-operation

Local authorities often have much the same interests and problems as their counterparts in other countries, and promoting transfrontier co-operation between them has always been one of the Assembly's concerns. The European Outline Convention on Transfrontier Co-operation between Territorial Communities or Authorities, opened for signing on 21 May 1980, was originally its proposal – in Recommendation 470 (1966). Its work in this area owed much to Karl Ahrens (Germany) and Louis Jung (France), successively its presidents in the 1980s.

■ **Signing of the European Convention on the Suppression of Terrorism,**
Palais de l'Europe,
27 January 1977.

Saving heritage

As early as 1970, the Assembly decided that more should be done to protect Europe's heritage, and that national laws needed harmonising for that purpose. It spelt out a programme in Recommendation 612 (1970), and gave that text more weight by appending a draft outline law, embodying general principles. The 1975 European Charter of the Architectural Heritage was a later product of this initiative. However, the Assembly wanted a full Council of Europe convention, and came back to the question in 1979. Its efforts contributed to the Convention for the Protection of the Architectural Heritage of Europe, which was opened for signing in 1985.

Protecting animals

The Assembly's work was behind several treaties in this field. The subjects covered were: protection of farm animals; transport and protection of animals for slaughter; protection of pet animals; wildlife conservation; and protection of vertebrate animals used for experimental and other scientific purposes. All these texts roused great public interest – particularly the last, which specialised NGOs wanted to make tougher, and which actually sparked demonstrations in Strasbourg and several member states.

As early as 1970, the Assembly felt that Europe's heritage needed more protection, and that national laws should be harmonised for that purpose.

"EUROPE'S DEMOCRATIC CONSCIENCE"

The Assembly feels that its character and membership imply a duty to serve as a "beacon of democracy", and act as "Europe's

"Beacon of democracy", "Europe's democratic conscience" – labels which reflect the Assembly's conception of its role.

democratic conscience". It believes that its task is not merely to promote and strengthen democracy and democratic institutions in the member states – but to spread democratic ideals outside Europe too.

As an "ideas laboratory" and a forum for discussion and reflection, it is actively involved in the ongoing debate on democracy – its nature, definition, workings and development. It considers these questions regularly, and it also responds to specific challenges, such as falling electoral turnouts or the threat of terrorism.

To give its work more impact in home parliaments, and back the efforts made by its member delegations, it seeks to involve the presidents/speakers of parliaments by organising regular European conferences for them at the Council of Europe.

Another of its tasks is to provide a parliamentary forum for the Organisation for Economic Co-operation and Development (OECD), which was founded in 1960. It does this by organising annual debates – attended by parliamentary delegations from Australia, Canada, Korea, Japan, Mexico, New Zealand and the United States – on the state of the world economy and the role of the OECD.

This openness to the outside world was reflected in the three major conferences on parliamentary democracy which the Assembly organised in Strasbourg in 1983, 1987 and 1991, and which offered a chance to look at the problems, and discuss approaches to strengthening and promoting parliamentary democracy. They also produced the "Strasbourg Consensus", which defines the essential components of pluralist, parliamentary democracy.

The European Conferences of Presidents of Parliament

Two conferences were organised in 1963 and 1973 bringing together presidents/speakers of parliaments of the member states (and the European Parliament). On 7 May 1974, to mark the Organisation's 25th anniversary, Assembly President Giuseppe Vedovato invited the presidents (speakers) of Council of Europe parliaments to a round table in Strasbourg. The theme was "The crisis of parliamentary democracy", and the participants urged the Assembly to make the most of its role as the guardian of democracy and human rights.

A further conference was held in Rome in 1975 at European Community (EC) level. Assembly President Karl Czernetz was there, and it was decided that the presidents (speakers) of Council of Europe and EC parliaments would attend future meetings on the same footing. From 1981 on, however, two types of conference were held: on the one hand, conferences of the presidents/speakers of EC parliaments and the European Parliament, and on the other, enlarged conferences. The latter are biennial, held under Assembly auspices, and attended by presidents/speakers from member states, observer countries and international assemblies.

The Assembly's openness to the outside world helped it to organise three major conferences on parliamentary democracy, in 1983, 1987 and 1991.

These "European parliamentary summits" provide a forum for wide-ranging discussion. Issues covered include: co-operation between national parliaments and the Parliamentary Assembly; the role of national parliaments in the European process;

The Assembly – source of ideas, beacon of democracy

human rights protection; supervision of governments by parliaments; measures aimed at combating organised crime and corruption; and action against terrorism.

The Strasbourg Conferences on Parliamentary Democracy

The presidents/speakers had expressed concern regarding democracy in Europe. The Assembly responded by making this the subject of a series of meetings at which parliamentarians and experts discussed themes which included: the development of democratic institutions in Europe (1976), the role of political parties (1978), technology and democracy (1981), and the concept of democracy (1983).

The 1976 conference, for example, noted that the role of parliaments was being downgraded in most Council of Europe member states, that parliaments were finding it increasingly hard to exercise their legislative powers and effective control over government, and that democratic institutions needed adjusting to bring them into line with the needs of modern societies. The topics it discussed included: the growing predominance of political parties; extra-parliamentary forces and pressure groups which threatened to subvert traditional patterns of representative democracy; more effective supervision of governments by parliaments; judicial control procedures; education policies geared to the promotion of equal opportunity, democratic beliefs and democratic behaviour; and the special role of the media as a democratic counter-force. Bruno Kreisky, the Austrian Chancellor, felt that democratic states outside Europe should also be able to attend. Speaking in the Assembly on 5 May 1976, he suggested that the OECD should

The European Conferences of Presidents of Parliaments, held every two years under Assembly auspices, come close to being "parliamentary summits".

have a political counterpart – a discussion forum for representatives of the world's democracies – and that the Council of Europe should work towards taking on that role.

At the January 1979 session, the Netherlands Foreign Minister, Chris van der Klaauw, asked a vital question: *"What does democracy mean in this our present time? Can we define it?"* Referring to the statement in the preamble to the ECHR, that fundamental freedoms are *"best maintained by an effective political democracy"*, he suggested that the Assembly attempt *"a definition, or if not a definition, an indication of the parameters of the notion of democratic society"*.

In September 1981, at the prompting of Assembly President José María de Areilza, who agreed that this issue should be tackled in a parliamentary forum, the Assembly's Bureau decided to organise a first "Strasbourg Conference" on parliamentary democracy. The Committee of Ministers' Swiss Chairman, Foreign Minister Pierre Aubert, supported the project, which he saw as matching the Council of Europe's need to ally itself with parliamentary democracies in other parts of the world, and also its political mission.

Speaking in the UK parliament in June 1982, US President Ronald Reagan gave the Strasbourg Conference his backing. In a message to the participants, Margaret Thatcher hailed it as *"an important and timely initiative"*, and added: *"The Parliamentary Assembly has always played a leading role in the Council of Europe's advancement of individual freedom, political liberty and human rights: it is particularly well-suited to the organisation of this new venture."*

The 1976 conference noted that the importance of the role played by parliaments in most Council of Europe member states was diminishing.

> In September 1981, the Assembly's Bureau decided to organise a first "Strasbourg Conference" on parliamentary democracy.

The conference took place in Strasbourg from 4 to 6 October 1983, and was attended by participants from the 21 Council of Europe countries, Israel and San Marino (both of which had observer status with the Assembly) and six OECD states outside the Council – Australia, Finland, Japan, Canada, New Zealand and the United States – in other words, nearly all the 30 or so recognised democracies existing in the world at that time.

As Assembly President Karl Ahrens declared: *"This is not the time or place to start out on a 'crusade' for democracy – but it seems to me necessary to reflect on the patterns of our collective national and political life in order to put our own house in order and keep it so"*.

The two themes discussed were "Parliamentary democracy today: answers to new challenges" and "Strengthening and promoting parliamentary democracy: common tasks". The aims were: to explore ways of helping democracy to function more effectively, to strengthen ties between the world's limited number of democracies, and to provide assistance for emergent democracies that needed it.

Alongside the conference, in a packed Assembly Chamber, young people from 14 countries held a parallel public meeting of their own. Most of them were students, and their priority concerns were action to relieve the plight of minorities – linguistic, ethnic or religious – and ensure respect for society's unwilling outsiders.

The Assembly – source of ideas, beacon of democracy

■ **Karl Ahrens, President of the Assembly from 1983 to 1986,** *speaking in the Chamber,* 1983.

Speaking at the first Strasbourg Conference (4-6 November 1983), Karl Ahrens declared: "This is not the time or place to start out on a 'crusade' for democracy – but it seems to me necessary to reflect on the patterns of our collective national and political life in order to put our own house in order and keep it so".

The 1st Strasbourg Conference produced the "Strasbourg Consensus", which defines the essential principles of pluralist parliamentary democracy.

The 2nd Strasbourg Conference (28-30 September 1987) was the largest-ever gathering of elected representatives from democracies worldwide. The opening address was delivered by French President François Mitterrand, who declared: *"I have always set great store by your institution and its work, and I think nearly all our countries would do well to draw more inspiration from it. […] The progress of democracy is what your Assembly is working for. […] You have no power to legislate, but you possess moral authority; the right to advise remains inviolable, as you have never ceased to affirm. We owe much to you for the furthering of democracy."* The discussions, led by Assembly President Louis Jung, focused on "democratic participation" and "education for democracy". One result of the second conference was the setting-up of the International Institute for Democracy, which functioned in Strasbourg from 1990 to the end of 2004.

The 3rd Strasbourg Conference (16-18 September 1991) was chaired by Assembly President Anders Björck, and attended by 500 participants from 90 countries. It took place at a time of radical upheaval, both in Europe and in many other parts of the world. Reflecting this context, its main theme was "Emerging or newly restored democracies – strengthening of democratic institutions and development". In their Final Declaration, the participants expressed their conviction that *"at this historic time, the peoples of the world are demanding the replacement of the formal concept of legality by the more meaningful concept of 'legitimacy'"*. In their view, genuinely legitimate political regimes could exist only in an international context which satisfied a number of conditions, one being recognition of the fact that *"human rights are no longer the exclusive province of states"* and that their infringement *"entails an actual duty of intervention"*.

They went on: *"Even if experience has shown that the poorest countries can achieve a viable democratic system – thereby demonstrating that democracy is fully compatible with all degrees of development – there is a need to promote a true partnership between the democracies of the North and South, to reduce the debt burden, in the name of interdependence and social justice, in order to strengthen emerging democracies and bring about a world based on a new ethic of international relations."*

The concepts of "legitimacy of political regimes" and "an international duty to intervene in defence of human rights" later became vital elements in a new conception of the international community.

The three Strasbourg conferences attracted great interest in Europe and outside, and did much to enhance the Assembly's prestige. However, lack of funds – and the need to give priority to expansion of the Council of Europe – made it impossible to take the series further.

■ **François Mitterrand, President of the French Republic,** *addressing the Assembly,* 1989.

The Assembly – source of ideas, beacon of democracy

Parliamentary forum for the OECD

The Assembly's annual debates on the "OECD and the world economy" are regularly attended by that organisation's Secretary General, and have been a notable success – particularly since they attract parliamentary delegations from non-European democracies which belong to the OECD, such as Australia, Canada, New Zealand, Japan and (with some delay) Korea. For a long time, these countries attended as observers only. This anomaly was corrected in the early 1990s, when an "enlarged Assembly" – operating within the normal one's framework, but with its own rules and procedure – was established. Within this new structure, all delegations, whether or not they come from Council of Europe states, enjoy the same rights.

Over the years, this annual meeting established itself as the broadest parliamentary forum for discussion of the world economy and of the OECD's role by the democracies – and helped to increase the international impact of both the Assembly and the Council of Europe. Sending parliamentary delegations made "overseas" governments aware of the Council and its work. As a result, Canada, Japan, Mexico and the US successfully applied in quick succession for observer status with the Council – and the Canadian and Mexican parliaments were given observer status with the Assembly too.

Conversely, the debates soon made the Assembly more aware of the Third World's problems and of underdevelopment. This message was also driven home by the Committee on Economic Affairs and Development which, under its Chairman Uwe Holtz

■ **Anders Björck, President of the Assembly** *from 1989 to 1991.*

(Germany), called for a new economic order, based on fairer distribution of wealth, greater social justice and protection of the environment. Similarly, in a report presented by Leni Fischer, Bundestag MP and future Assembly President, the Committee on Culture and Education insisted that education for development must be promoted, and Europeans made aware of North-South interdependence and the need for solidarity. In 1989, the Assembly took its work in this area further by launching a Europe-wide public campaign on that very theme. This produced some important results: that same year, the Committee of Ministers set up the European Centre for Global Interdependence and Solidarity (better known as the "North-South Centre") in Lisbon. In effect, the centre (with which the Assembly has a co-operation agreement) is pioneering North-South dialogue for the Council of Europe.

CHANGE IN THE EAST

After the world's brush with disaster at the time of the Cuban missile crisis (1962), there were signs of a thaw in East-West relations – and the Assembly started to wonder whether the Council of Europe's co-operation system could not be extended beyond its actual membership. It was clear that the Eastern bloc countries could not join, either because they were wary of the Council's political activities, or because they fell short of its criteria. The Assembly's thinking on this question was coloured by the work of its Committee on Relations with European Non-Member Countries, which studied attitudes and trends in the East and

These annual meetings – the broadest-ever forum for parliamentary discussion of the world economy – increased the international impact of both the Assembly and the Council of Europe.

The Assembly – source of ideas, beacon of democracy

1989 saw the Assembly's campaign for North-South interdependence and solidarity and the founding of the Council of Europe's North-South Centre in Lisbon.

assessed the prospects for multilateral co-operation with the West. It reported signs of change in the East, where some countries were keen to preserve their relative autonomy within the Communist bloc, while others hoped that the Soviet Union's new policy of peaceful co-existence might give them more scope for foreign policy initiatives. Fears of a widening technological gap with the West were another important factor. In Recommendation 389, adopted in April 1964, the Assembly declared that the Council of Europe had a duty *"to contribute at the same time towards the unification of a free and democratic Europe and the easing of tension which has begun between East and West"*, and encouraged the member states *"to find forms for a genuine peaceful co-existence between the Soviet Union on the one hand, and a Europe in the process of unification and the United States on the other"*. A year later, in Recommendation 412 (1965), it asked the Committee of Ministers to urge member states to develop their commercial and cultural ties with Romania and the other east European countries. Many political analysts backed the Council of Europe's approach, feeling that its brand of multilateral co-operation might give the eastern countries what they wanted, even if joining was still not an option. The period from 1967 to 1969 saw visits to Warsaw and Belgrade by the Council of Europe's Secretary General, Peter Smithers, and to Bucharest by the Assembly's outgoing President, Geoffrey de Freitas.

In 1968, the Assembly held a major debate on peace research. The report which served as its starting point discussed proposals that the Council of Europe's Statute be amended, so that east

European countries could join. It also suggested that the Assembly admit Communist MPs from member states' parliaments – which it did in 1973. Finally, it suggested abolition of the Committee on Relations with European Non-Member Countries, which some eastern countries thought excessively critical.

Nascent ties with the East were sorely tested that same year, when Warsaw Pact forces invaded Czechoslovakia. The Assembly condemned this move unreservedly and expressed *"its solidarity with the oppressed Czechoslovak people"*.

Nonetheless, several east European countries later attended Council of Europe meetings on issues such as demography, monuments and the environment. Yugoslavia took part in activities concerned with school and higher education, and was granted observer status with the Conference of Local and Regional Authorities of Europe (the future Congress) in 1970. Contacts were restricted to technical questions for some years, but this did nothing to invalidate the Assembly's general approach, which proved itself triumphantly later – and particularly after 1989.

The Assembly – political forum for East-West co-operation

Between 1967 and 1978, many heads of government and foreign ministers spoke on East-West relations and the CSCE in the Assembly. Their statements reflected their open approach to these issues – and the role they envisaged for the Council of Europe.

Speaking in the Assembly on 24 January 1967, Willy Brandt, Vice-Chancellor and Minister for Foreign Affairs of the Federal

The Assembly – source of ideas, beacon of democracy

On 28 January 1975, Milos Minic, Deputy Prime Minister and Minister for Foreign Affairs of Yugoslavia, declared in Strasbourg: "All the European countries have the momentous responsibility of making a decisive contribution, thanks to their […] behaviour in concrete situations, not only to understanding and co-operation in Europe but also to understanding and co-operation between all European countries and the non-aligned and developing countries".

Milos Minic, Deputy Prime Minister and Minister for Foreign Affairs of Yugoslavia, *addressing the Assembly, under the gaze of Assembly President Giuseppe Vedovato, 28 January 1975.*

Republic of Germany (FRG), expounded his country's east European policy and canvassed the Assembly's support for it. He considered that: *"Our continent will be able to attain the desired state of peace only when the gap which separates East from West has been bridged. The division of Europe hinders the development of its intellectual and economic capacities and weakens its role and its possibilities in the world of today"*.

Taking his argument further, he declared: *"Our object is the strengthening of co-operation with the east European peoples and states in the technological, scientific and cultural fields – and, when and where possible, in the political field as well. Co-operation of the kind I have described is the touchstone of détente in our part of the world. In certain spheres, and between certain partners East and West, a compromise of conflicting interests can be achieved. Making the most of our very limited scope for doing that is the task of a European policy of détente. And if we succeed, we may well set in train developments which will one day make compromise possible in spheres where it is unattainable today."*

On 25 January 1971, Austrian Chancellor Bruno Kreisky voiced his country's interest in Recommendation 614 (1970), which urged the Committee of Ministers to keep the question of East-West relations, and the organisation of one or more European security conferences, on its agenda, and consider both the setting-up of a permanent body for East-West co-operation and the Council of Europe's contribution in this context. He went on: *"Political questions apart, co-operation in scientific, cultural*

A 1968 report discussed proposals for amendment of the Statute, so that east European countries could join – and suggested admitting Communist MPs from member countries.

Willy Brandt, Federal German Vice-Chancellor and Foreign Minister, explained his country's *Ostpolitik* and sought the Assembly's support for it.

and technological fields is of particular importance in contacts between countries of Western and Eastern Europe. In these fields specifically, the Council of Europe has made a valuable breakthrough."

Speaking in the Assembly on 16 May 1973, Giulio Andreotti, President of the Italian Council of Ministers, expressed his conviction that the Council of Europe should *"play a part, to the fullest extent possible, in the process of détente in which we are involved and which finds today its most concrete expression in the preparations for the Conference on Security and Co-operation in Europe"*. He went on: *"Perhaps at the start we cannot hope for too much in this regard, but it would be useful to investigate whether and how the Council of Europe might constitute a meeting place for engaging in activities of a technical nature which are of interest to the countries of Eastern and Western Europe alike. The Council's competence and practicality are recognised and appreciated even beyond the frontiers of the Seventeen and that should encourage us not to give up our pursuit of this goal."*

Addressing the Assembly on 27 January 1976, as Chairman of the Committee of Ministers, Federal German Foreign Minister Hans-Dietrich Genscher declared: *"It seems quite natural to me that the Council of Europe should now be concerned to see how the Final Act of the Helsinki Conference can be translated into reality. After consulting its partner governments, the Federal Government called for an intensive exchange of views within the Committee of Ministers and the Ministers' Deputies. A successful start has since been made with this. What already applied during the long years of negotiation in Geneva and Helsinki should continue to apply now in implementing the decisions of the Conference: consultation within the Atlantic Pact and among the Nine should be continuously supplemented by discussions between all the European democracies, united in the Council of Europe."*

Helmut Schmidt, the German Chancellor, spoke in the Assembly on 27 April 1978. He urged the Council of Europe to play an active part in preparing the Madrid Conference, scheduled for 1980, and to co-ordinate its efforts with the nine Community states. He declared: *"Before this Assembly, which comprises parliamentary representatives of most of the states taking part in the CSCE, I should like to make one point: I am convinced that the CSCE process, which is a decisive factor in multilateral détente throughout Europe, is so important for the future – and not only the future of our continent – that we cannot afford to limit it to technical details and the swapping of position papers."*

The Assembly and the CSCE

In March 1969, the Warsaw Pact countries proposed holding a conference on pan-European security. Two months later, the Committee of Ministers expressed the view that multilateral contacts between the Council of Europe and the Eastern bloc countries on legal, cultural, educational and other technical issues could indeed contribute to détente in Europe. The Assembly responded by organising several debates on this question and, in Recommendation 597 (1970), asked the Committee to *"adopt a*

"Co-operation in scientific, cultural and technological fields is of particular importance in contacts between countries of Western and Eastern Europe." Bruno Kreisky, January 1971.

Helmut Schmidt, the German Chancellor, urged the Council of Europe to get involved in preparing the Madrid Conference, and co-ordinate its efforts with the Community countries.

positive attitude towards the idea of one or several European security conferences" and *"make full use of the possibilities provided by the Council of Europe as an instrument for political and technical consultation and action"*. However, meeting in Budapest in June 1970, the Warsaw Pact foreign ministers asked the future conference to consider setting up a special body to deal with security and co-operation in Europe – and various proposals for an "organisation of European states" also came from the West. In Recommendation 614 (1970) the Assembly voiced its fear that a new agency might duplicate work already done by existing organisations. Once the CSCE's Final Act was signed (1 August 1975), it set about monitoring the signatories' compliance with their obligations – the subject of regular debates from May 1976 on.

The CSCE's lack of a parliamentary dimension made this even more necessary. The Assembly, on the other hand, covered nearly all the west European democracies (including the neutrals) – and had decided to involve Finland and the parliaments of the five non-European states which already attended the debates on the OECD.

In the 1970s, the Assembly forged closer links with the Yugoslav Parliament. From 1972 on, Yugoslav parliamentarians attended its conferences and hearings, and its President, Giuseppe Vedovato, visited Belgrade officially in 1973. On 28 January 1975, Milos Minic, Yugoslav Deputy Prime Minister and Minister for Foreign Affairs, told the Assembly: *"All the countries of Europe have a duty to contribute decisively, through their understanding of contemporary historical processes and their conduct in specific situations, to understanding and co-operation, not just between European countries, but also between European countries and the non-aligned and developing countries, with a view to establishing new economic and political relations, based on international equality, and to strengthening peace and security in the world."* Answering questions, he added that the Council of Europe could play a bigger role in achieving better relations between eastern and western Europe.

In 1976, the Council of Europe's Secretary General, Georg Kahn-Ackerman, went to Belgrade, and Yugoslavia signed three conventions on higher education. Between 1978 and 1980, various members of the Yugoslav Parliament were invited to meetings of the Political Affairs Committee.

But the Assembly's efforts to develop its relations with other east European countries were hampered by the war which broke out in Afghanistan in 1980.

THE ASSEMBLY AND THE UNITED NATIONS

In the 1960s, the Assembly – led by its President, Pierre Pflimlin – worked to build closer relations with the United States, and with the Latin American and African countries. It also turned towards the United Nations (UN), with which the Council of Europe concluded a co-operation agreement in 1951. In its January 1965 general policy debate, it discussed the UN's financial crisis and affirmed its support for the organisation. On 3 May 1966, the UN

The Assembly was afraid that a new agency might duplicate the work of existing ones.

In the 1970s, the Assembly forged closer links with the Yugoslav Parliament, and Yugoslav parliamentarians attended its conferences and hearings from 1972.

Secretary General, U Thant, came to Strasbourg. Speaking in the Assembly, he declared that the Council of Europe had *"given a most significant lead to other regions of the world"* in the human rights field, and *"built on the broad initiatives of the United Nations"*. He went on: *"It is encouraging to note its increasing contacts with the countries of Eastern Europe, which are not members of the Council. In recent years, regional organisations have come to be more clearly regarded as complementary to the world organisation, rather than as substitutes for it. The work of regional organisations and the United Nations should be concerted, not competitive. Moreover, in a world that lives so dangerously, we must all be constantly on the alert to avoid any act or policy which would, in fact, serve divisiveness rather than unity in the relations between nations and peoples."* He gave the Assembly a vivid account of the divisive factors – particularly those which seriously threatened relations between peoples, and fuelled tensions. *"It is, in my view, the growing economic disparity of the nations of the world which faces us with our most serious source of tension and with the direct possibility of future calamity. [...] We must now concert and vastly strengthen our efforts to bridge this widening economic gap, no matter what the discouragements, the frustrations or the problems may be. [...] The countries of Europe, united in this and other organisations, have a particularly favourable position from which to promote the concerted action which the world so urgently needs and to mobilise expertise and resources on the scale which the size and seriousness of the problem demand."* He concluded: *"I am sure that the Council of Europe, representing the European spirit at its* best, will show increasingly how Europe, which used to be called the old world, can be among the leaders of the new."*

His successor, Kurt Waldheim, addressed the Assembly in May 1976. He declared: *"The Council of Europe is a pioneering experiment in international co-operation. The common political, historical and cultural background of its members gives it initial advantages denied to more broadly based international organisations. It is a highly sophisticated venture in international co-operation and, as such, it is watched with great interest in the world at large. Some of its features – its human rights machinery for example – are important developments in international organisation. The work of regional groupings is, I am convinced, an essential and valuable element in developing an articulate approach to world affairs and in dealing with global problems. The existence of such groupings unquestionably facilitates the working of the United Nations. Without them, and with its present all but universal membership, the proceedings of the world organisation would be more difficult to manage."*

ADOPTING A WORK PROGRAMME, HELPING YOUNG PEOPLE

The Council of Europe's first intergovernmental work programme was launched in 1966. The Assembly has contributed to this from the start, always trying to align it on the actual needs of Europeans, and to extend it to new sectors, for example the environment, co-operation in the youth field, regional planning, sport, science and technology, heritage, etc.

The Assembly – source of ideas, beacon of democracy

> "In the field of human rights, you have given a most significant lead to other regions of the world. [...] It is encouraging to note your increasing contacts with the countries of Eastern Europe, which are not members of the Council."

U Thant, UN Secretary General,
*in Strasbourg,
3 May 1966.*

It has been behind, or involved in, various "years" and campaigns: European Nature Year (1970), European Architectural Heritage Year (1975), the Countryside Campaign (1987-88), the youth campaigns, European Music Year (1985).

Above all, however, it has focused on finding solutions to Europe's major social problems. A particularly striking example came in the late 1960s, when disenchantment with consumer values gripped the universities, triggering a protest movement which later spread to industry, with students and workers making common cause. In France, things came to a head in May 1968, when violent demonstrations rocked the cities, and a general strike paralysed the country.

The Assembly and its Committee on Culture and Education responded by tackling the root issues in a series of debates, on "The present crisis in European society" (24 September 1968), "The role of universities in relation to the world of economics and politics" (1 October 1969) and "Co-operation in the youth field" (26 January 1970). On all three occasions, Marcel Hicter (Belgium) represented the Council for Cultural Co-operation. Director of the Belgian Culture Ministry's youth services, he was not only an expert on youth problems, but also a dazzling speaker, and he held the Assembly spellbound. Subjecting the causes of the protests to a penetrating analysis, he declared: *"The extent, scope and breathtaking speed of the scientific discoveries that are turning our production methods upside down mean that the world is being flooded with new processes which are already transforming it utterly and revolutionising our traditional*

"The Council of Europe is a pioneering experiment in international co-operation",
Kurt Waldheim, UN Secretary General.

productive and social structures, as well as the material foundations of human life. [...] Every new generation must realise that its whole life will be a series of upheavals. Adaptability, versatility, readiness to change – these are the prime virtues which we need to instil in the young. The crisis of youth is a crisis of civilisation, and total reform of contemporary society is the only key to resolving it. [...] Post-industrial civilisation and the scientific and technical revolution will create a gulf between the educated and the uneducated. [...] Humanising the living environment is the only way of making community life itself possible."

The Council of Europe adopted its first intergovernmental work programme in 1966. The Assembly has contributed to this from the start.

In his view, there were two main objectives: *"to give people an education that will enable them to share in change and adjust to it, as part of a life-long process co-ordinating all the factors that contribute to their development"* and *"to give people a socio-cultural environment which will stimulate and enrich them, while fostering their personal development and interest in others"*. He was convinced that the crisis could be overcome if society would only take young people more seriously and give them a genuine role. He suggested that the Council of Europe should act, and that the European Youth Centre – which the Council for Cultural Co-operation was operating on a trial basis – should be made permanent, and progress from merely studying the problems of young people to actively preparing them for life in a fast-moving world.

The third debate brought a proposal from Heinz Westphal, German Secretary of State for Young People and Families, who suggested that a European Youth Office, modelled on the Franco-

■ **Youth Assembly,**
organised by the Parliamentary Assembly,
30 April 1999.

German Youth Office established by the Elysée Treaty in January 1963, should be set up at the Council of Europe – and insisted that young people from east and south-east Europe must be involved in its work.

The upshot of all this discussion was Recommendation 592 (1970), which contributed decisively to the setting-up of two specialised youth agencies at the Council of Europe, in 1971 and 1972 respectively: the European Youth Centre, a residential facility which provides training for members of non-governmental youth organisations, and the European Youth Foundation, which funds youth activities in the member states and beyond. Both are co-managed by youth organisations and governments.

The centre and foundation developed rapidly, and played a notable part in providing European training for leading members of youth organisations (political, trade union, educational and ecological). Several future members – and two future presidents – of the Assembly took part in their activities.

> "The crisis of youth is a crisis of civilisation, and total reform of contemporary society is the only key to resolving it",
> Marcel Hicter, 26 January 1970.

7

Expanding in the West, opening to the East

"It is time to consign to oblivion the Cold War postulates."

■ **Mikhail Gorbachev, President of the Supreme Soviet of the USSR,** *speaking in the Assembly,* 6 July 1989.

Expanding in the West, opening to the East

Community enlargement made it necessary for the Council of Europe to redefine its role and activities.

The Assembly's work from 1980 to 1989 had three main objectives: to complete its membership in western Europe; to find a modus vivendi with the European Community, which was admitting new members and extending the range of its activities; to intensify its contacts with the countries of eastern Europe, encouraging them to forge closer ties with the Council of Europe and its democratic values.

Once Portugal (1976) and Spain (1977) had joined, the Assembly decided to approach three small and hitherto neglected states: Liechtenstein, San Marino and Andorra. It also tried more persuasive tactics on the only sizeable country which still, for geopolitical reasons, deferred joining – Finland.

At the same time, progressive enlargement and institutional reform of the Community, which wanted a "Citizens' Europe" based on a Single Act, made it necessary for the Council of Europe to redefine its role and the scope of its activities. The Assembly, which wanted to link the Council of Europe and European Community processes, gave this question its special attention, making it the subject of fruitful dialogue with the Committee of Ministers.

Finally, the Council of Europe needed to find its place in the process of East-West rapprochement, which was developing within the Conference on Security and Co-operation in Europe (CSCE). The Helsinki Final Act, signed in 1975, was followed by numerous international conferences, including those in Madrid (1980-83) and Vienna (1986-89), which led, in 1990, to the signing of the Charter of Paris for a New Europe, and to the CSCE's becoming a permanent organisation, the Organization for Security and Co-operation in Europe (OSCE).

The problem for the Assembly in both cases was the same. In principle, it favoured anything which made for European unity and better East-West relations – but it was also determined to defend the Council of Europe's political role and its vital work in promoting human rights and democracy.

FULL HOUSE IN THE WEST

Liechtenstein

In 1971, when relations with European non-member countries were being discussed, the Bureau decided, at Assembly President Olivier Reverdin's proposal, to invite parliamentary representatives from Liechtenstein to attend debates on matters of interest to that country – but without giving them any special status or committing the Assembly. It was not until November 1974, under the presidency of Giuseppe Vedovato (Italy), that the Assembly's Standing Committee decided to grant observer status (introduced in 1961) to Liechtenstein, as *"a democratic European state, solely responsible for the conduct of its foreign relations, which is represented at the CSCE in this capacity and already sends a representative to Assembly sessions by invitation"*.

The Liechtenstein Government applied for Council of Europe membership in November 1977. Gerhard Reddemann (Germany)

■ **Liechtenstein joins**
Georg Kahn-Ackermann (right), Secretary General of the Council of Europe, congratulates Liechtenstein Prime Minister Hans Brunhart, Strasbourg,
23 November 1978.

reported favourably for the Political Affairs Committee, and Toby Jessel (United Kingdom) did the same for the Committee on Relations with European Non-Member Countries, and the Assembly adopted Opinion No. 90 (1978), noting that Liechtenstein was an independent and sovereign European state, belonged to various international organisations, had signed the Final Act of the Conference on Security and Co-operation in Europe, and had a constitution and laws *"founded on the principles of human rights and fundamental freedoms as embodied in the European Convention on Human Rights"*. Its one complaint – although the country's only women's political organisation favoured Council membership – was that women were still denied the right to vote in general elections and referendums.

This was enough for the Committee of Ministers, and Liechtenstein joined the Council of Europe on 23 November 1978. In July 1984, it responded to the Assembly's earlier criticism by extending the franchise to women. In 1987, it chaired the Committee of Ministers for the first time.

San Marino

The Parliament of the Republic of San Marino was granted observer status with the Assembly in 1982.

On 18 January 1988, its government applied to join the Council of Europe. The two rapporteurs – Gerhard Reddemann of the Political Affairs Committee and Daniel Tarschys of the Committee on Relations with European Non-Member Countries (a future Council of Europe Secretary General) – supported the application, regarding San Marino

In July 1984, Liechtenstein responded to Assembly criticism by giving women the vote.

as a sovereign, democratic state, and noting that it had taken due account of the Assembly's observations on gender equality and media pluralism. On that basis, the Assembly gave a favourable opinion. San Marino became a member on 16 November 1988, and went on to chair the Committee of Ministers in 1990.

Andorra

The government of San Marino applied to join the Council of Europe on 18 January 1988.

Andorra's case was complicated by the fact that sovereignty was exercised, for historical reasons, by two co-princes, the Comte de Foix (whose successor today is the President of France) and the Spanish Bishop of Urgel. Robert Pontillon (France) and Lluís Maria de Puig (Spain) visited the country in April 1989, to research a report for the Assembly on prospects for its joining. In that report, they noted that Andorra had undergone *"a profound economic, social and demographic transformation"* in recent decades, but that, despite some reforms, its political institutions had failed to keep pace with these developments, *"as a result of which Andorra can scarcely be regarded as a modern state based on the rule of law"*. They further noted that *"full enjoyment of civil and political rights, the heritage of the Council of Europe's member countries, is problematical for all those who are subject to Andorran jurisdiction, whether as citizens or as mere residents"*, and concluded there could be *"no question at present of contemplating Andorra's accession to the Council"*. Taken together, the reports of the Political Affairs Committee, the Committee on Legal Affairs and Human Rights and the Committee on Relations with European Non-Member

Countries gave a detailed picture of the country's history and political, legal and institutional development.

The Assembly's debate on Andorra was attended by Andorran representatives and several Spanish parliamentarians. One of the latter was Miguel Ángel Martínez, a future Assembly President and former exile under Franco, who recalled that his father – otherwise forbidden to leave Spain – had often contrived to visit him in Andorra. At the end of the debate, the Assembly urged the co-princes to allow the country to affirm its sovereignty, and bring its political institutions into line with democratic requirements and the realities of its rapid social and economic development. In Resolution 946 (1990), it suggested that Andorra adopt a written constitution, make existing institutions the basis of a genuine parliament and government, reform its electoral law and ease the rules on naturalisation, so that foreign residents – who already outnumbered natives – could gradually be absorbed. In the meantime, in Resolution 947 (1990), the Assembly decided to encourage Andorra's *"continuing presence and participation"* in Council of Europe activities, and, in Recommendation 1127 (1990), asked the Committee of Ministers to join the Andorran authorities in selecting Council of Europe conventions which Andorra could immediately accept.

The Andorran Government completed the reforms the Council had asked for, and applied for membership on 22 November 1993. In Opinion No. 182 (1993), the Assembly welcomed the coming into force (4 May 1993) of the new constitution, which installed the rule of law, and guaranteed human rights and

The Assembly urged the co-princes to allow Andorra to bring its institutions into line with democratic requirements.

fundamental freedoms. It noted that parliamentary elections, based on direct, universal suffrage, had been held on 12 December 1993, with an 81% turnout – and observed by an ad hoc Assembly committee, which had judged them free, democratic and lawful. It asked the Andorran Government to accede to the principal Council conventions, including the European Convention on Human Rights and the European Social Charter.

Andorra was formally admitted to the Council of Europe on 10 November 1994.

Finland

Finland's first links with the Council of Europe date back to 1970, when it ratified the European Cultural Convention. Moreover, since 1976, Finnish MPs had been taking part in the Assembly's annual enlarged debates on the activities of the OECD, and attending specialised Assembly meetings, such as the Strasbourg Conferences on Parliamentary Democracy, the first of which took place in 1983.

Finland's links with the Council of Europe date back to its acceptance of the European Cultural Convention in 1970.

Contacts with Finland were strengthened in May 1987, when the Conference of European Ministers of Education was held in Helsinki, and again in May 1988, when the Secretary General responded to the Finnish Government's decision to start negotiating membership by going to the country on an official visit.

On 27 May 1988, Finland formally applied to join the Council of Europe, and two Finnish parliamentarians were present when the Assembly discussed its application on 1 February 1989. The Political

Affairs Committee reported favourably, emphasising Finland's outstanding parliamentary and international traditions, and noting that it identified wholeheartedly with the West, while itself symbolising the Helsinki Process. It also noted that its joining would make the Council's membership co-extensive, for the first time, with the "European democratic area". Some doubts regarding Finland's legal system were removed by its promise to sign the ECHR on joining, and its determination to apply Council of Europe standards and introduce any reforms needed to comply with them.

Finland became a member on 5 May 1989 – the day on which the Council of Europe celebrated its 40th anniversary.

THE COUNCIL OF EUROPE'S FUTURE ROLE – FOCUS FOR DIALOGUE BETWEEN THE ASSEMBLY AND THE COMMITTEE OF MINISTERS

As early as 1972, the Assembly asked its Political Affairs Committee to set up a working party to consult member governments and parliaments, and report to it on what the Council of Europe should be doing in the new situation created by the European Community's recent first enlargement, which had taken its membership from six to nine (the newcomers were Denmark, Ireland and the UK). The committee's report was prepared by Olivier Reverdin, a former Assembly president, and circulated to the member states. The Assembly discussed it on 16 May 1973, and adopted Recommendation 704 (1973) on the mission of the Council of Europe, which laid down guidelines for co-ordination of the Organisation's activities with those of the Community. It

Finland joined the Council of Europe on 5 May 1989 – the Organisation's 50th anniversary. In its report, the Political Affairs Committee paid tribute to its outstanding parliamentary and international traditions, and noted that it identified fully with the West, while also symbolising the Helsinki Process. Its joining made the Council's membership co-extensive, for the first time, with the "European democratic area".

■ **The Finnish flag is raised**
*at the Council of Europe,
5 May 1989.*

also emphasised that the Council of Europe offered the best forum for East-West co-operation, and for work on the themes which were central to its mission: human rights and the harmonisation of law; culture, education and youth; the impact of scientific and technological progress; the natural and man-made environment in relation to regional planning; scientific policy and basic research; social rights, public health and consumer protection; and the role of local authorities.

Concerning relations between the Council of Europe and the European Community, the Assembly recommended that the Committee of Ministers:

"a. *invite member governments, particularly the governments of the Nine, to co-ordinate the activities of the Council of Europe and of the Community, having due regard to the role and resources of each, without drawing a hard and fast line between their respective activity sectors, and applying the following criteria*

> *– geographical criterion: the Council of Europe must be empowered to deal with all questions which transcend the geographical boundaries of the Community;*

> *– methodological criterion: the Council of Europe must be given preference in matters which are not suited to integration by the Community methods;*

b. *use its meetings to foster dialogue between members and non-members of the Community, on the basis of a progress*

Recommendation 704 (1973) made the point that the Council of Europe was the best platform for East-West co-operation.

report of the Community's Council of Ministers and a report on co-operation within the Nine on matters of foreign policy;

c. *time its ministerial meetings so that some of them are held immediately after meetings of the foreign ministers of the Community countries;*

> The Assembly insisted that the Council of Europe must be empowered to deal with any question which transcended the Community's boundaries.

d. *ensure continuous and effective liaison between the Community and the Council of Europe, at ministerial and parliamentary level, and between the various departments of the Commission and the Secretariat General;*

e. *set up a Council of Europe office in Brussels and ask the Community to appoint a mission to the Council of Europe."*

Most of these points were taken over by the Committee of Ministers in Resolution (74) 4 on the future role of the Council of Europe, which it adopted on 24 January 1974.

In 1976, Belgian Prime Minister Leo Tindemans submitted a report to the European Council on a future "European Union", and on the first direct elections to the European Parliament, scheduled for June 1979. The Assembly reacted at once by commissioning a report from Swiss MP Pierre Aubert, which was discussed at the October 1977 session. In Recommendation 821 (1977), it noted *"discordance in European co-operation, with the institutions being encouraged to compete rather than to act in concert"*, and insisted that closer relations with the EC were needed to keep Europe's parliamentary democracies united on the basis of shared values and principles. It welcomed the up-grading of the European Parliament's democratic legitimacy – a legitimacy which it, too, possessed as a parliamentary body based on the national parliaments of numerous European countries.

In May 1982, the Committee of Ministers asked its Chairman-in-Office, Austrian Foreign Minister Willibald Pahr, to produce a paper on the Council of Europe's future role. Part of the background to this was the draft European Act jointly prepared by the German and Italian Foreign Ministers, Hans-Dietrich Genscher and Emilio Colombo, which contained proposals on a step-by-step approach to European union, particularly in the cultural and legal fields – where the Council had been active from the start, with very tangible results. Willibald Pahr suggested a "gentlemen's agreement", giving the Council of Europe (which then had 21 member states) preference whenever better results could be achieved in a broader European context.

The Assembly returned to these issues when it discussed the "general policy of the Council of Europe – European co-operation in the 1980s", on the basis of a report by Norwegian MP Harold Lied. In Resolution 805 (1983), it called for *"unremitting efforts to achieve greater complementarity, reciprocity, coherence and effectiveness"* in relations with the European Communities. It was anxious that the Council of Europe, with its broader mandate and larger membership, but more limited resources, should contribute to the essential task of revitalising Europe, and ensure that its own members did not divide into Community and non-Community groupings, with possibly disastrous results for the whole of democratic Europe.

The Assembly noted that the European institutions were being encouraged to compete, not co-operate.

It decided *"to intensify its own independent reflections on the future of European co-operation"*. For this purpose, it set up a *"commission of prominent statesmen"* from Community and non-Community countries, who were to sit in an individual capacity and consider this whole question.

The Committee of Ministers asked its Chairman to come up with ideas on the Council of Europe's future role.

The Assembly also tackled the question of East-West relations. It was concerned at *"the lack of official relations between the Council of Europe and the majority of Eastern European countries"*, and urged the Committee of Ministers to explore the possibility of their participating in the Council's intergovernmental work in such fields as culture, education and the environment. It also asked the Committee to discuss *"political questions affecting European East-West relations"* at regular intervals and report to it.

The European Community continued working on the question too. In June 1984, the European Summit at Fontainebleau decided to set up two ad hoc committees – one on institutional affairs, chaired by James Dooge on behalf of the Irish Prime Minister, Garret Fitzgerald, the other on "People's Europe", chaired by Pietro Adonnino, a former Italian MP – to make proposals on improving co-operation in Europe. On 3 October 1984, on the basis of a report presented for the Political Affairs Committee by Harold Lied, the Assembly adopted Recommendation 994 (1984) on the future of European co-operation, determining the membership and mandate of the "Commission of Eminent Statesmen", which was to be chaired by Emilio Colombo, a former Italian Foreign Minister.

Declaring that the Council of Europe could not content itself with "the role of spectator" in this area, the Assembly stipulated that the commission should liaise with the two above committees.

It was not entirely happy with the EC's plan for a people's Europe, and insisted that the Council of Europe's work should be taken into account, and that co-ordination and consultation should precede any crucial decisions. Finally, it decided to strengthen its ties with the European Parliament, which had been elected by universal suffrage for the second time in June 1984, and had appointed former Assembly President Pierre Pflimlin (France) to its presidency.

The Colombo Commission

Recommendation 994 (1984) named eight members: Emilio Colombo, Chairman, former Italian Foreign Minister; José María de Areilza, a former Spanish Foreign Minister and ex-President of the Assembly; Piet Dankert, a former President of the European Parliament and ex-member of the Assembly; Maurice Faure, a former French Minister and ex-member of the European Parliament; Knut Frydenlund, a former Norwegian Foreign Minister and ex-member of the Assembly; Kai Uwe von Hassel, a former Minister and ex-President of the Bundestag and the WEU Assembly; Alois Mock, Austrian Chairman of the International Democratic Union; and Geoffrey Rippon, a former UK Foreign Secretary.

The Colombo Commission's task was to make proposals on ways of *"strengthening the co-operation between all the democratic states of Europe, in order to avoid a widening gap between*

The Council of Europe's lack of official relations with most of the east European countries was a cause of concern to the Assembly.

Expanding in the West, opening to the East

Emilio Colombo (left),
Chairman of the Colombo Commission,
with Marcelino Oreja, Secretary General
of the Council of Europe,
Palais de l'Europe,
28 January 1984.

them", and produce *"bold and realistic suggestions"*, covering major areas of the lives of Europeans, that might help to bring about *"a fully united Europe"*.

It was also asked to *"look into the adequacy of existing European institutions"*, with reference to *"the realities and requirements of the Europe of tomorrow"* and present long-term proposals, as well as proposals which could be implemented at once, for the benefit of Europeans. It was told that it *"should keep in mind the broader prospective of Europe, encompassing more than the Western European democracies"*.

The interim report

On 12 June 1985, the commission submitted an interim report to the President of the Assembly, the Chairman of the Committee of Ministers and the Secretary General of the Council of Europe. It acknowledged that more members and increased powers had turned the European Community into the *"central dynamic element in the process of European unification"*, but warned against *"the very grave risk – for the family of European democratic states – of a widening of the gap already existing between members of the Community and the other members of the Council of Europe"*. It insisted that the ties between these two groups of states must be strengthened by developing *"mechanisms of co-operation"* between the European Community and the Council of Europe, particularly in the fields of: political dialogue, parliamentary democracy, human rights protection, social problems (terrorism, drugs, unemployment, especially of the young, pollution), cultural identity, migration, education and training, research, science and technology, harmonisation of law, and regional and local authorities. It recommended that the Community participate fully in multilateral co-operation at the Council of Europe, and accede to its legal instruments (primarily the ECHR) and even the Statute.

In Recommendation 1017 (1985), the Assembly endorsed most of the Colombo Commission's initial proposals and asked the Committee of Ministers to write them into the Council of Europe's intergovernmental work programme for 1986.

The final report

The Colombo Commission submitted its final report in June 1986. This again insisted that close co-ordination and co-operation between the Council of Europe and the European Community held the key to their shared aim of strengthening solidarity in Europe, and referred to Article 230 of the Treaty of Rome, which states that *"the Community shall establish all appropriate forms of co-operation with the Council of Europe"*. It responded favourably to various proposals in the Adonnino Report – particularly the suggestion that the European Community adopt the Council of Europe's symbols – the European flag and anthem.

Concerning "the other Europe", the commission considered that dialogue in the cultural field was *"of paramount importance in maintaining, developing and deepening the links which transcend the present division of our continent"*. The only basis for lasting peace in Europe was *"continuous political dialogue, as well as bilateral and multilateral co-operation between all*

The Colombo Commission's job was to come up with ideas and suggestions on strengthening co-operation between Europe's democracies.

European states". Because of its membership and the nature of its activities, the Council of Europe was ideally placed to promote co-operation between economic and political systems across the East-West divide – which was why it must seek co-operation with European non-member countries in areas which fell within its remit and concerned the whole of Europe.

The Colombo Commission declared that strengthening solidarity in Europe depended on close co-ordination and co-operation between the Council of Europe and the European Community.

Council of Europe and European Community – reaching an "arrangement"

The Council of Europe regarded a full and formal agreement with the two major Europe-building institutions as the best option. What it got, on 16 June 1987, was an "arrangement" – spelt out in an exchange of letters between its Secretary General, Marcelino Oreja, and the President of the EC Commission, Jacques Delors. These letters formalised practical details of co-operation between the two sides, and gave effect to the recommendations made by the Colombo Commission and the Assembly, and to Committee of Ministers Resolution (85) 5 of 25 April 1985. To encourage the Community to participate in the Council's work, they provided for regular exchanges of information, participation by senior officials from each institution in the activities of the other, and systematic consultation in areas of common interest. More specifically, the Secretary General of the Council of Europe was to consult the EC Commission on organising joint activities, and the EC Commission was invited to send representatives to all expert committee meetings and ministerial conferences held at the Council of Europe.

The Parliamentary Assembly and the European Parliament also stepped up their co-operation by making it easier for committee chairs and rapporteurs to attend meetings of their counterpart committees in the other institution, and maintaining regular contacts between their secretariats.

THE COUNCIL OF EUROPE LOOKS EAST

Throughout this period, the Assembly regularly called for intensified East-West dialogue, détente and co-operation. Thus, in Recommendation 498 – adopted on 26 September 1967, when hostilities had broken out in the Middle East – it insisted that, in the interest of peace, *"co-operation between the member states of the Council of Europe and the Soviet Union and the other states of Eastern Europe must be encouraged"*, and urged the Committee of Ministers *"to neglect no opportunity of promoting co-operation between East and West"*. At its meeting in May 1969, the Committee of Ministers expressed its conviction that multilateral contacts between the Council of Europe and eastern Europe in the technical, legal and cultural fields could contribute effectively to détente.

Encouraged by progress made with the CSCE process, the Assembly exerted further pressure in favour of new links with the East. In Resolutions 805 (1983) and 826 (1984), it urged the governments of member states to *"intensify European co-operation in the various specialised fields of activity included within the general terms of reference of the Council of Europe, and particularly in the educational, cultural, economic, environmental, legal*

Expanding in the West, opening to the East

In Resolutions 805 (1983) and 826 (1984), the Assembly urged member governments to intensify East-West relations in the various specialised fields covered by the Council of Europe's general mandate. The idea that Europe's shared cultural identity could serve as a basis for East-West co-operation, and help to overcome political antagonisms, was also gaining ground. This new approach owed much to the efforts of Hans-Dietrich Genscher, Federal German Foreign Minister and Chairman-in-Office of the Committee of Ministers, and Marcelino Oreja, the Council of Europe's Secretary General, who met in Bonn several times in November and December 1984.

Hans-Dietrich Genscher, Federal German Foreign Minister, and Chairman-in-Office of the Committee of Ministers, *addressing the Assembly, 1984.*

and scientific fields". The idea that Europe's shared cultural identity could serve as a basis for co-operation, and help to overcome political antagonisms between East and West was steadily gaining ground.

This new approach owed much to the efforts of Hans-Dietrich Genscher, Federal German Foreign Minister and Chairman-in-Office of the Committee of Ministers, and the Secretary General, Marcelino Oreja, who held several meetings in Bonn in November and December 1984. Together, they discussed areas – particularly culture – where co-operation with the East could be intensified, and fixed a preliminary timetable for contacts with a number of east European countries, starting with Yugoslavia, Hungary, Czechoslovakia and Poland. These bilateral meetings were followed, in January 1985, by a special ministerial meeting on East-West relations. The Committee of Ministers adopted Resolution (85) 6, in which it instructed the Deputies to *"ascertain and propose areas where it would be possible to engage in closer co-operation with those states of Europe that are neither members of the Council of Europe nor parties to the European Cultural Convention, and to report back to the Committee of Ministers on this matter"*.

On 7 October 1987, the Council of Europe's open-door policy led to Yugoslavia's acceding to the European Cultural Convention, giving it the right to participate fully in the Council's intergovernmental activities in the fields of culture, education, sport and youth. Yugoslavia had actually been sending observers to various intergovernmental committees since 1975, and had been admit-

The Assembly wanted intensified dialogue, détente and co-operation between East and West.

ted to several conventions, particularly those concerned with recognition of diplomas.

Parliamentary diplomacy

The special ministerial meeting had instructed the Secretary General to visit various east European countries. While he was doing this, the Assembly was itself making high-level contacts with Hungary, Poland, Romania, Czechoslovakia and the USSR, as well as Bulgaria and the German Democratic Republic (GDR). The aim of this diplomatic exercise was to sound out possibilities for closer ties between the Council of Europe and eastern Europe – the constant concern of the Committee on Relations with European Non-Member Countries, which was set to play a key role in the extension of the Organisation.

In October 1987, Assembly President Louis Jung was invited to Bucharest by the President of the Romanian Grand National Assembly. The aim of the visit was to explore prospects for cooperation, but the human rights situation and Romania's plans for "land regularisation" (actually the suppression of 7 000 villages chiefly inhabited by Hungarians) were also discussed. A delegation from the Grand National Assembly, led by its President, returned the visit in June 1988.

In April 1988 a delegation from the Supreme Soviet of the USSR came to Strasbourg for talks with the Assembly, particularly its President and enlarged Bureau. It was agreed that the two bodies could work together under the following headings: general cooperation, politics, environment, culture and education, health

More and more people were convinced that Europe's shared cultural identity could help to bridge the political divide.

and legal affairs. The Soviet press agency TASS hailed this as *"highly significant and genuinely historic"* and *"the start of a wholly new era in the development of relations between Soviet and West European parliamentarians"*. A second visit took place in October 1988. In the meantime, the Assembly's Standing Committee had decided, at its meeting in Athens on 30 June, to invite Mikhail Gorbachev, Secretary General of the Soviet Communist Party since March 1985, and soon to succeed Andrei Gromyko as President of the Supreme Soviet, to address the Assembly.

In February 1985, an Assembly delegation, led by the President, was invited to Belgrade. In October, for the first time, a Yugoslav parliamentarian spoke in the Assembly's annual debate on the activities of the OECD. In June 1986, a Yugoslav delegation attended the Political Affairs Committee's meeting in Innsbruck. In April 1988, the Assembly's President went to Yugoslavia (including Kosovo) with representatives of the political groups and the Chairman of the Committee on Relations with European Non-Member Countries. Next to visit was the Secretary General, in November, and Yugoslavia began to play a bigger part in the Council of Europe's intergovernmental activities and the work of the Assembly, which awarded it special guest status on 8 June 1989. On 7 February 1990, it applied for full Council membership, but a very different process was already starting to unfold at home: relations between Kosovo's Albanian majority and the power-wielding Serbian minority were worsening, and other republics were starting to resent Serbia's high-handed dominance of the federal system. A draft

The Assembly made high-level contacts with Hungary, Poland, Romania, Czechoslovakia and the USSR, as well as with Bulgaria and the German Democratic Republic.

> In April 1988, the Supreme Soviet of the USSR sent a delegation to Strasbourg for talks with the Assembly.

report on Yugoslav accession was prepared for the Political Affairs Committee, the Legal Affairs Committee and the Committee on Relations with European Non-Member Countries. The rapporteurs, including future Assembly President Miguel Ángel Martínez, concluded that Yugoslavia should be brought into the European integration process, and specifically the Council of Europe, once free elections had been held in the republics and autonomous provinces, and the country had promised to ratify the ECHR (including its optional clauses) with no territorial reservations. But Yugoslavia was moving towards implosion, and the report never reached the Assembly.

May 1984 saw the first contacts with Hungary, when the Vice-President of the Hungarian Parliament visited the Assembly. In June 1987, the Council of Europe's Secretary General, Marcelino Oreja, met the Hungarian Foreign Minister and the Minister for Culture and Education in Budapest. In May 1988, at a meeting with members of the Political Affairs Committee and the Committee on Relations with European Non-Member Countries, the Hungarian Secretary of State for Foreign Affairs, Gyula Horn, struck a promising note when he hinted that substantial improvements in the matter of human rights and democracy could be expected. In November 1988, the President of the Assembly went to Hungary, following a meeting of the Committee on Relations with European Non-Member Countries in Budapest – the first time that an Assembly committee had met in an east European country.

During this same period, parliamentarians and experts from these countries, and also Bulgaria and the GDR, took part in various Assembly activities.

East-West relations and the CSCE

The Assembly held major debates on East-West relations in September 1986, September 1987 and October 1988. The first two were introduced by the Norwegian MP Harold Lied, and the third by the French MP Catherine Lalumière, later Secretary General of the Council of Europe. Knowing that East-West negotiations within the CSCE had a powerful impact on the Council's scope for action, the rapporteurs paid special attention to this process. Indeed, there were those who hoped that the Assembly might yet become the CSCE's parliamentary arm, and this was openly suggested at the Assembly's meetings in Innsbruck at the end of June 1990. There were two arguments in favour: firstly, the CSCE needed a democratic dimension, and secondly, the Assembly could provide it – if American and Canadian parliamentarians were suitably involved in its work. It so happened that President George Bush had much the same idea at the NATO Summit in London that July, when his proposal for a European Assembly based on the Council of Europe's was written into the Final Declaration. Relying on US backing, the Assembly started preparing to host a debate on security and co-operation in Europe, attended by parliamentarians from all the CSCE member states. The real situation soon become plain, however. The US Congress was against the project, and boycotted the first debate

In April 1988, the President of the Assembly went to Yugoslavia (including Kosovo) with representatives of the political groups. The Yugoslav Parliament was awarded special guest status on 8 June 1989.

The President of the Assembly went to Hungary, after a meeting of the Committee on Relations with European Non-Member Countries in Budapest – the first time that an Assembly committee had met in an east European country.

in September 1990 – although a number of Canadian parliamentarians did attend.

The third of the Assembly's earlier debates on East-West relations had been preceded by the Gorbachev/Reagan Summit, which led to a reduction in nuclear (but not conventional) weapons in December 1987, and the Soviet withdrawal from Afghanistan in April 1988. This double breakthrough, and Gorbachev's new policy of glasnost (openness) and perestroika (reorganisation) accounted for the optimistic tone of the debate – partly offset by continuing distrust of Soviet Union intentions in some quarters and frustration at repeated setbacks within the CSCE. Presenting her report, Catherine Lalumière declared: *"The Council of Europe, established in the aftermath of a war to unite democracies around common values, is clearly in the best position to examine and clarify those values, which have been put to the test by modern developments and disappointments, in order to ascertain what remains of them at the end of the 20th century. The Council is also best placed to explore, with the countries of Eastern Europe, the potential for a European awareness, a European identity, a 'common European home', first with one country, then with another, until it finally extends from the Atlantic to the Urals"*. She warned that excessive optimism and undue caution must both be avoided. Peter Schieder, Austrian parliamentarian and future Assembly President, insisted on the opportunities offered to the Council of Europe and declared: *"It is said that, in old age, nothing hurts as much as missed opportunities. This is probably true not only of individuals, but also of peoples, states and international organisations. We must seize opportunities when they present themselves. The importance of the well-timed initiative as an ingredient of events is probably still underestimated"*. In Resolution 909 (1988), the Assembly resolved to *"pursue and intensify its existing contacts with the European non-member countries, in order to establish effective structures and machinery for dialogue aimed at better mutual knowledge and co-operation towards détente and European unification in the broader sense"*. It also called on the Committee of Ministers *"to maintain the new momentum of pan-European relations"*.

That same year, the Committee on Culture and Education organised a round table on the role which young people could play in forging closer ties between East and West, involving parliamentarians and representatives of youth organisations from eastern Europe. The conclusions, presented by, among others, a future Assembly President, Lord Russell-Johnston, stressed the importance of youth mobility for East-West understanding, and insisted that young people – natural champions of peace, human rights and social justice – could do much to change attitudes. The work done at this round table helped to pave the way for the opening of a second European Youth Centre in Budapest (1995).

The Pope's appeal (8 October 1988)

A number of Assembly members suggested that inviting the Pope to Strasbourg would effectively bolster the Council of Europe's policy of openness to the East. The idea was an instant

Some people hoped the Assembly might become the CSCE's parliamentary arm.

"The Council of Europe is best placed to explore, with the countries of eastern Europe, the potential for a European awareness, a European identity, a 'common European home'". Catherine Lalumière, October 1988.

success. John Paul II's charisma, commitment to healing East-West division in Europe, and dedication to working for peace worldwide had earned him a universal reputation. He was also the head of a state, the Holy See, which had signed the European Cultural Convention in December 1962, and had been taking part in Council of Europe activities ever since, appointing a permanent mission to the Council in the early 1970s. He addressed the Assembly on 8 October 1988. In his speech of welcome, Assembly President Louis Jung declared: *"Here we try to work according to principles which are a part of the foundations of the Christian religion. […] We know about your efforts to foster brotherhood among all men, but do you also know about the great mission which this Assembly has assigned itself by working to bring all Europeans closer together? We believe that dialogue with leaders from all countries of this continent will make action possible to remove the barriers imposed by war and by force."*

John Paul II started by paying a resounding tribute to the Council of Europe and its founders: *"Your Council has the great and fine vocation of bringing the nations of this continent closer together in order to consolidate peace based upon justice, for the preservation of human society and civilisation, in an unshakable commitment to the spiritual and moral values which are the common heritage of their peoples."* He went on: *"It is fitting that we should pay tribute to the clear-sighted men who contrived to meet across frontiers, to set aside old enmities, to propose and bring to fruition the project of this Council, destined to become a place where Europe may achieve self-*

awareness, where it measures the tasks it needs to accomplish in response to the anxieties and the expectations of its citizens, for it undertakes necessary co-operation in many arduous fields". He declared his support for the Council of Europe's efforts to reunite the continent: *"If Europe wishes to be true to itself, it must contrive to gather together all the live forces of this continent […]. The member countries of your Council are aware that they are not the whole of Europe; in expressing the fervent wish for intensification of co-operation, already sketched out, with other nations, particularly in central and eastern Europe, I feel that I share the desire of millions of men and women who know that they are linked by a common history and who hope for a destiny of unity and solidarity on the scale of this whole continent."*

He concluded: *"In coming here today, before the world's first-ever international Parliamentary Assembly, I am aware that I am addressing the qualified representatives of peoples who, loyal to their vital origins, wished to join together to consolidate their unity and to open their arms to other nations of all continents, in respect for the truth of man. I can bear witness to the willingness of Christians to take an active part in the work of your institution. I wish for your Council that it may work fruitfully in order to make Europe's soul ever more living and generous."*

Expanding in the West, opening to the East

Pope John Paul II addressed the Assembly on 8 October 1988. "If Europe wishes to be true to itself, it must contrive to gather together all the live forces of this continent [...]. The member countries of your Council are aware that they are not the whole of Europe; in expressing the fervent wish for intensification of co-operation, already sketched out, with other nations, particularly in central and eastern Europe, I feel that I share the desire of millions of men and women who know that they are linked by a common history and who hope for a destiny of unity and solidarity on the scale of this whole continent."

His Holiness Pope John Paul II, *addressing the Assembly, in the gaze of President Louis Jung (right), 8 October 1988.*

1989 – THE TURNING POINT

On 5 May 1989, the Council of Europe celebrated its 40th anniversary, and Finland became its 23rd member state. Now that it included nearly all the states of western Europe, the Council was starting to set its sights on the states of central and eastern Europe – cautiously at first, later more boldly. Basically, it was waiting for developments and decisions in the East which would allow it to put the Assembly's open-door policy, and concomitant plans for enlargement, into effect. The situation cleared in 1989, in every sense a watershed year for the Council – and for Europe.

Mitterand speaks out

On 5 May 1989, the Assembly welcomed another special visitor – François Mitterand, the host country's President. Taking European cultural identity as his opening theme, he called on the members to persist in their efforts to secure closer ties with the countries of central and eastern Europe:

"All Europeans – whether they belong to the part of Europe which is represented here today or to the other part – share a common destiny. History proves it, and geography does too. There must be a genuine political determination to move in that direction. The things I have just said about audiovisual media apply equally well to what we loosely and misleadingly call the eastern countries. After all, East and West both have a North and a South. Moreover, the 'Western' countries are not all in the

Pope John Paul II backed the Council of Europe's efforts to reunite the continent.

Expanding in the West, opening to the East

On 5 May 1989, the Council of Europe celebrated its 40th birthday – and Finland became its 23rd member.

West, nor the 'Eastern' countries in the East. Still, little as I like them, those terms are understood, and so I have used them too.

I know there are contacts, and that you yourselves have made some of them, via the Parliamentary Assembly or intergovernmental co-operation. There are ventures involving Hungary and Poland, and your Assembly has established contacts with the Soviet Union. It is my belief, and France's too, that the time has come to forge new, closer and groundbreaking links between these two Europes, whenever events make this possible, by moving in the direction envisaged by the Council of Europe's founding fathers – the direction of freedom.

No one must feel excluded from this great movement, which will, I am convinced – without wishing to prophesy – be the making of Europe in the next millennium. There is near-scientific evidence that peoples who hold together stand every chance of enduring, developing and winning through if they only acknowledge their affinities.

The Council of Europe can press ahead with bold co-operative initiatives, involving its members and any others who wish to join in them. Responding to the expectations of those, wherever they may be, who cherish freedom and who, like us, see themselves as the heirs and inhabitants of the same Europe, is – and this is not something I am teaching you, but something you have taught me – one of the Council of Europe's primary functions.

The Council of Europe, and all of us, must respond to the divisions born of war by generously offering a community of culture and exchange, as a basis for further progress later. In the short term, why not review the requirements for observer status or envisage new ways of involving the states of the other Europe, on conditions which you will naturally have to determine?

The historian Fernand Braudel once spoke (he was thinking of France, but the image seems apt here) of 'a readiness to follow wherever the wind blows' – and that seems to me to chime well with the spirit of your institution. A little poetry never hurt anyone."

Special guest status

His words gave fresh heart to the many who felt that the time had come to move faster, and particularly the Committee on Relations with European Non-Member Countries, which had been thinking for some months about "special guest status" as a way of formalising the Assembly's contacts with certain non-member parliaments. Without further ado, it now finalised that project.

This was a total innovation, covered neither by the Council of Europe's Statute nor the Assembly's Rules of Procedure – and it showed that the parliamentarians could still pull a rabbit from the hat when they had to. Special guest status was limited to the Assembly, and it gave selected non-member delegations the right to sit in the chamber, speak in debates and take part in the work of committees, but not to vote. It was aimed at parliamentarians from European non-member countries which respected the CSCE instruments and the United Nations covenants of 1966 on civil

François Mitterrand urged the parliamentarians to keep working for closer ties with eastern Europe.

Expanding in the West, opening to the East

and political rights. "Special guest" parliaments were required to send pluralist delegations, whose credentials were checked – and could be contested – like those of member delegations.

"Responding to the expectations of those, wherever they may be, who cherish freedom and who, like us, see themselves as the heirs and inhabitants of the same Europe, is one of the Council of Europe's primary functions", François Mitterrand, 5 May 1989.

Swiss MP Peter Sager, Chairman of the Committee on Relations with European Non-Member Countries, presented its report on special guest status to the Assembly on 11 May 1989. The day before, the committee had had an exchange of views with Solidarność leader Lech Walesa – in Strasbourg to receive the European Human Rights Prize at the Council of Europe. Peter Sager declared: *"The fact that yesterday was the first time, to my knowledge, that this august Assembly has had the opportunity to hear a speech in a Slav language suggests to me that we are fully attuned to the historic importance of the era through which the Council of Europe is passing in the 40th year of its existence."* After a very fruitful phase of parliamentary diplomacy, he suggested that the time had come to *"embark on a new stage of co-operation, for which the institutional foundations have already been laid"*. He hailed this as a new and historic departure for the Council of Europe, and went on: *"It is true that this first step will not bridge the gulf between Eastern and Western Europe – far from it. All the same, we may be certain that we are effectively initiating a process of rapprochement. The road ahead will be a long one, but the stages on it will reflect great humanitarian advances: consolidation of democracy, reinforcement of the rule of law, respect for human rights"*.

Sir Geoffrey Finsberg, rapporteur to the Political Affairs Committee and the Committee on Rules of Procedure, who went on to become President of the Assembly in 1992, struck the same note. Referring to Winston Churchill, he said: *"His concept of one Europe, represented by a Council of Europe, is beginning to come to fruition. We now have 23 member countries and are looking one stage further. We are, of course, the only possible organisation that can do this. I do not believe that anyone with any understanding or common sense would deny that"*. At the same time, he quoted the Latin adage: *"Festina lente"*, and declared: *"We must go forward step by step […]. Understandably, special guest status must be earned and it must be carefully controlled. […] What is important is not merely the signing of the conventions and resolutions but their implementation."*

All the speakers knew that they were seeing the dawn of a new era, heralding some of the most important changes in the history of humanity. Some warned, however, that the Council of Europe must beware of losing its soul, and must not compromise its credibility by accepting lower human rights standards in central and eastern Europe.

At the end of the debate, Ludwig Steiner (Austria), Chairman of the Political Affairs Committee, declared: *"Today sees the beginning of a new chapter in the activity of the Parliamentary Assembly, which has shown its capacity and its will to tread new paths. […] We naturally hope that the current pattern of developments in Eastern Europe will continue. We know, of course, that the point of no return has not yet been reached,*

Expanding in the West, opening to the East

Solidarność leader Lech Walesa received the European Human Rights Prize at the Council of Europe on 10 May 1989, and had an exchange of views with the Committee on Relations with European Non-Member Countries. Speaking in the Assembly, Peter Sager suggested that its having, for the first time, heard a speech in a Slav language put it fully in tune with "the historic era" which the Council was traversing as it celebrated its 40th anniversary. After a fruitful phase of parliamentary diplomacy, he felt the time had come to "embark on a new stage of co-operation, for which the institutional foundations have already been laid".

Solidarnośc leader Lech Walesa, *in the Assembly, 10 May 1989.*

but I believe we should not be frightened by our own daring, and should bravely tackle our task, with enthusiasm, idealism and patience. In doing so, we should always remember our own principles – principles which we must and will not abandon, and which must not be available to our guests at costs lower than those applying to observers or full members".

Special guest status was formally introduced on 11 May 1989, and already awarded in June to the parliaments of Hungary, Poland, the Soviet Union and Yugoslavia, whose delegations took part in the Assembly's debate on East-West relations in July. The scheme's full potential was revealed when the Berlin Wall came down (November 1989), and the Eastern bloc ceased to exist. The quickening pace of events had taken western Europe by surprise, but special guest status with the Council of Europe gave it a first response to the pressing demands of countries thirsting for democracy. The next special guests were Czechoslovakia (May 1990), Bulgaria (July 1990) and Romania (February 1991). Estonia, Latvia and Lithuania followed in September 1991, and Albania in November that same year. Indeed, all the Council's new members since then have been special guests to start with. The Parliament of the GDR was briefly on the list – from March 1990, when the first free elections were held, until October, when Germany was reunited.

6 July 1989: Gorbachev and the "common European home"

Mikhail Gorbachev – apostle of détente, co-operation and peaceful coexistence (he won the 1990 Nobel Peace Prize for

"We are fully attuned to the historic importance of the era through which the Council of Europe is passing in the 40th year of its existence", Peter Sager, 12 May 1989.

Expanding in the West, opening to the East

Some speakers warned that the Council of Europe must not lose its soul, or jeopardise its credibility by lowering its standards.

withdrawing Soviet troops from Afghanistan) – puzzled and fascinated people in the West. His groundbreaking style, totally at odds with his Moscow predecessors' dogged adherence to the status quo, appealed to the Assembly. When its Standing Committee suggested inviting him to Strasbourg, the idea struck many observers as a bold one – and some governments accused the Council of Europe of jumping the gun. Nonetheless, the invitation was duly formalised on 31 October by Assembly President Louis Jung.

Moscow responded with interest, but some caution. Without actually saying no, the Kremlin preferred to wait and think the matter over. The pros and cons were discreetly discussed behind the scenes and, on 19 April 1989, Gorbachev accepted. On 6 July, he came to Strasbourg to expound his vision of the "common European home".

For the first time, an east European head of state – and not just any head of state, but the President of the Supreme Soviet of the USSR – was speaking in the Assembly, with representatives of 23 western countries and, also for the first time, special guest delegations from Hungary, Poland, the USSR, the GDR and Yugoslavia in attendance. This gave added weight to the point made by Assembly President Anders Björck when he declared: *"The Council of Europe's task cannot be considered to have been completed until our continent has been rid of the division inherited from the war, which separated peoples sharing a common cultural heritage and a European identity."*

Mikhail Gorbachev detailed his vision of a *"common European home"*: a shared home built on shared foundations – the rule of law, respect for human rights, economic liberalism and a shared cultural identity – but with each tenant free to arrange their own part of it.

He called for *"a vast economic space from the Atlantic to the Urals, where Eastern and Western parts would be strongly interlocked"*, and *"a European legal space"*, and urged European states to familiarise themselves with one another's cultures. He reaffirmed the existence of two distinct social models: *"The fact that the states of Europe belong to different social systems is a reality. Recognition of this historical fact and respect for the sovereign right of each people to choose their social system at their own discretion are the most important prerequisite for a normal European process."*

The very next day, the Assembly held a current affairs debate on East-West relations – the perfect opportunity for a wide-ranging exchange of views on this question, and particularly Gorbachev's speech. There were 35 speakers on the list. Karl Ahrens, Gerhard Reddemann, Geoffrey Finsberg and Peter Sager spoke respectively for the Socialist Group, the European People's Party, the European Democrat Group and the Liberal, Democratic and Reformers' Group. The chairmen of the special guest delegations from Hungary, Poland, the USSR and Yugoslavia also spoke. Their contributions were in keeping with the importance of the issues, and the whole debate was a shining example of European parliamentarianism in action. It

Special guest status was introduced on 11 May 1989 – and awarded to the parliaments of Hungary, Poland, the Soviet Union and Yugoslavia a month later.

was clear that things were starting to move in the East – and in the West too. Alfonse d'Amato, a representative of the US Congress, was also present and declared: *"Let me speak plainly. I believe that the United States has an intrinsic interest in seeing that the Soviet Union and its allies identify with the house of freedom."* He also said: *"My immediate personal goal is to see that our President comes here, participates in this forum and delivers a speech of substance, as President Gorbachev did yesterday."* When all the speakers had had their say, the Assembly was left with the impression that a reunited Europe was no longer a mere pipe dream.

Mikhail Gorbachev intrigued and fascinated Westerners, and his pioneering break with the status quo in Moscow won him friends in the Assembly.

Jacques Delors in the Assembly (26 September 1989)

Jacques Delors was in Strasbourg for the last part of the Assembly's 1989 session – the first time that a President of the EC Commission had addressed it. He opened with a tribute to the Council of Europe: *"Whatever may have been the difficulties over the years, we cannot forget that it was with the Council of Europe that it all began, that it was with the Council of Europe that hope was born, here in this forum described by Robert Schuman as 'a laboratory where European co-operation is tested'."* He then expounded his conception of Council-Community relations, with complementarity as keynote: *"Although the Community and Council share the same aim – European unity – our fields of activity and our methods differ, as no doubt do our ambitions. This has to be said frankly. But the two institutions must complement each other, with the intergovernmental Council of Europe as the guardian and advocate of*

■ **Mikhail Gorbachev, President of the Supreme Soviet of the USSR,** *in the office of Anders Björck, President of the Assembly, 6 July 1989.*

The Standing Committee's decision to invite Mikhail Gorbachev to Strasbourg seemed very bold at the time – and premature to some governments. Speaking before the Assembly on 6 July 1989, he expounded his vision of a "common European home": a shared home built on shared foundations – the rule of law, respect for human rights, economic liberalism and a shared cultural identity – but with each tenant free to arrange their own living quarters.

Expanding in the West, opening to the East

democratic values throughout Europe, and the Community, which has chosen an integrationist policy, working for European union with all who unreservedly accept the full contract. I repeat: the full contract".

Replying to questions, he spoke of the Council of Europe's responsibilities in the field of East-West co-operation: *"The Council of Europe is today, I believe, the most appropriate framework for the construction of the Europe of tomorrow, in so far as you constitute the 'framework' or the 'space' in which a dialogue can be instituted unequivocally, cautiously and gradually.*

Jacques Delors' first visit was a highlight of the Assembly's last part-session in 1989.

From this point of view, the task of the Community is a different one. It may have bilateral relations with Yugoslavia, Poland and Hungary, but the Council of Europe is the discussion forum where we can best ascertain whether we share and respect certain values, and whether we all subscribe to the rules of international law.

I am sure that the initiatives you have taken will enable you to play this role. That is why I spoke about a beginning, the dialogue, which has already started here."

Before receiving Jacques Delors, the Assembly had been discussing the situation of refugees from central and eastern Europe, and its next sitting was devoted to reports on the problems of minorities in Romania and Bulgaria. In this watershed year of 1989, eastern Europe had soared to the top of its agenda – and the rest of the world would soon be feeling the impact as well.

The momentum increased as the end of the year drew near. Austria and Hungary opened their borders to GDR citizens seeking to leave and, at mass demonstrations in Leipzig and other major cities, the call for freedom and democracy was growing steadily louder. Finally, on 9 November, the Berlin Wall was breached, and Germans East and West joined hands beneath the Brandenburg Gate.

German reunification was unmistakably coming, and people East and West were starting to believe that European unity was not just a dream, but a real possibility. At last it seemed that the founding fathers' vision of the Council of Europe as a place where representatives of all the peoples of Europe would gather beneath a single roof was on the point of being realised. The second chapter in the Council's story was beginning – and the Assembly would again play a major part in writing it.

Fragment of the Berlin Wall
in front of the Human Rights Building, Strasbourg,
December 2005.

The Committee on Relations with European Non-Member Countries

In Resolution 14 of 28 August 1950, the Assembly recognised *"that certain nations which are precluded from participating in the work of the Council of Europe nevertheless form an integral part of Europe"*, and decided to set up *"a special committee whose duty it would be to ensure that the interests of these nations shall be considered in every proposal which may be formulated by the Assembly or its committees"*. This committee was authorised to *"request the advice of experts belonging to these nations"*.

In Resolution 105 of 25 October 1956, the Assembly decided to turn this special committee into a "committee on non-represented nations". This was given the task of examining questions of interest to the Iron Curtain countries, and considering whether they might participate in certain Council of Europe activities. The Assembly insisted that the new committee's permanent character did not mean that those countries were regarded as a lost cause, but was meant to ensure that they did not feel abandoned by the Council.

In accordance with its mandate, the committee reported on the situation and prospects of the central and east European countries, sought to promote cultural contacts with them, and recommended measures aimed at the release of political prisoners. One of its reports, debated in 1958, dealt with the "Assembly of Captive European Nations" (ACEN), comprising delegations of exiles and refugees from various communist countries: Albania, Bulgaria, Czechoslovakia, Estonia, Hungary, Latvia, Lithuania, Poland and Romania. Its main aims, according to its charter, were to work to free the captive nations of central and eastern Europe from communist dictatorship and Soviet domination, and affirm their right to be represented at the United Nations only by their own legitimate governments, based on the will of their respective peoples. When the ACEN asked to work with the Council of Europe on a political action programme, the committee replied, regretfully, that the Organisation's Statute made this impossible – but decided to maintain contact for information purposes.

In 1979, the committee was renamed the "Committee on Relations with European Non-Member Countries", reflecting the sense of détente generated by the Conference on Security and Co-operation in Europe. Chaired by parliamentarians who favoured closer East-West ties, like Peter Sager (Switzerland), regarded as one of the fathers of special guest status, David Atkinson (United Kingdom) and Jean Seitlinger (France), it played an important part in enlargement of the Council of Europe.

Once most of the central and east European countries had joined, however, its *raison d'être* largely disappeared. It was abolished in 1997, when the Committee on the Honouring of Obligations and Commitments by Member States of the Council of Europe (Monitoring Committee) was formed.

PRESIDENTS OF THE ASSEMBLY

1949	**Edouard HERRIOT** (Honorary President, 10-11 August) (France, Radical Party)
1949-1951	**Paul-Henri SPAAK** (Belgium, Socialist)
1952-1954	**François de MENTHON** (France, Christian Democrat)
1954-1956	**Guy MOLLET** (France, Socialist)
1956-1959	**Fernand DEHOUSSE** (Belgium, Socialist)
1959	**John EDWARDS** (United Kingdom, Socialist)
1960-1963	**Per FEDERSPIEL** (Denmark, Liberal)
1963-1966	**Pierre PFLIMLIN** (France, Christian Democrat)
1966-1969	**Sir Geoffrey de FREITAS** (United Kingdom, Socialist)
1969-1972	**Olivier REVERDIN** (Switzerland, Liberal)
1972-1975	**Guiseppe VEDOVATO** (Italy, Christian Democrat)
1975-1978	**Karl CZERNETZ** (Austria, Socialist)
1978-1981	**Hans J. de KOSTER** (Netherlands, Liberal)
1981-1983	**José Maria de AREILZA** (Spain, Conservative)
1983-1986	**Karl AHRENS** (FRG, Socialist)
1986-1989	**Louis JUNG** (France, Christian Democrat)
1989-1991	**Anders BJÖRCK** (Sweden, Conservative)
1992 (February to May)	**Sir Geoffrey FINSBERG** (United Kingdom, Conservative)
1992-1996	**Miguel Angel MARTINEZ** (Spain, Socialist)
1996-1999	**Leni FISCHER** (Germany, Christian Democrat)
1999-2002	**Lord RUSSELL-JOHNSTON** (United Kingdom, Liberal)
2002-2005	**Peter SCHIEDER** (Austria, Socialist)
2005-	**René van der LINDEN** (Netherlands, Christian Democrat)

CLERKS/SECRETARIES GENERAL OF THE ASSEMBLY

1949	**Lord Gilbert CAMPION** (10 August-8 September) (United Kingdom)
1950-1954	**Filippo CARACCIOLO DI CASTAGNETO** (Italy)
1954-1955	**Arnold STRUYCKEN** (Netherlands)
1955-1956	**Dunstan CURTIS** (United Kingdom), acting
1956-1971	**Gerhart SCHLOESSER** (Germany)
1971-1986	**John PRIESTMAN** (United Kingdom)
1987-1996	**Heinrich KLEBES** (Germany)
1996-2006	**Bruno HALLER** (France)

SECRETARIES GENERAL OF THE COUNCIL OF EUROPE

1949-1953	**Jacques-Camille PARIS** (France)
1953-1956	**Léon MARCHAL** (France)
1956-1957	**Dunstan CURTIS** (United Kingdom), acting
1957-1964	**Lodovico BENVENUTI** (Italy, Christian Democrat)
1964-1969	**Peter SMITHERS** (United Kingdom, Conservative)
1969-1974	**Lujo TONCIC-SORINJ** (Austria, Christian Democrat)
1974-1979	**Georg KAHN-ACKERMANN** (FRG, Socialist)
1979-1984	**Franz KARASEK** (Austria, Christian Democrat)
1984-1989	**Marcelino OREJA AGUIRRE** (Spain, Christian Democrat)
1989-1994	**Catherine LALUMIÈRE** (France, Socialist)
1994-1999	**Daniel TARSCHYS** (Sweden, Liberal)
1999-2004	**Walter SCHWIMMER** (Austria, Christian Democrat)
2004-	**Terry DAVIS** (United Kingdom, Socialist)

DEPUTY SECRETARIES GENERAL

1949-1952	**Aubrey S. HALFORD** (United Kingdom)
1952-1955	**Anthony H. LINCOLIN** (United Kingdom)
1955-1962	**Dunstan CURTIS** (United Kingdom)
1962-1968	**Polys MODINOS** (Cyprus)
1968-1978	**Sforza-Galeazzo SFORZA** (Italy)
1978-1993	**Gaetano ADINOLFI** (Italy)
1993-1997	**Peter LEUPRECHT** (Austria)
1997-2002	**Hans Christian KRÜGER** (Germany)
2002-	**Maud DE BOER-BUQUICCHIO** (Netherlands)

THE ASSEMBLY IN BRIEF

The Statute of the Council of Europe, adopted on 5 May 1949, established two bodies: the Committee of Ministers and the Assembly, which work together to realise the Organisation's aims. The Assembly is the Council's deliberative body. In accordance with the official declaration published when the Statute was signed: *"The Consultative Assembly will provide a means through which the aspirations of the European peoples may be formulated and expressed, the governments thus being kept continuously in touch with European public opinion."*

1. Composition

The Assembly comprises 315 representatives and the same number of substitutes. Its members are appointed by national parliaments.

2. Structure

President and Vice-Presidents

The President of the Assembly is elected yearly from among the members and, traditionally, may be reappointed twice. There are 20 Vice-Presidents, who are members of the Bureau.

National delegations

In the Assembly, each member state has a number of representatives determined by its population. Delegation size varies from 2 to 18.

At the beginning of each session, the Assembly ratifies the credentials of members appointed by national parliaments. The political make-up of each delegation must reflect, as faithfully as possible, the representation of the various parties in its home parliament.

Political groups

The Assembly has five political groups: the Socialist Group (SOC); the Group of the European People's Party (EPP); the Alliance of Liberals and Democrats for Europe (ALDE); the European Democrat Group (EDG); and the Group of the Unified European Left (UEL). Members of the Assembly are free to join the group of their choice.

Bureau

The Bureau of the Assembly comprises the President, 20 Vice-Presidents, the chairs of the political groups and the chairs of committees. It co-ordinates the work of the Assembly and its committees, adopts the agenda and prepares the session schedule; it decides on referring documents to committees and oversees the Assembly's external relations.

Standing Committee

The Standing Committee comprises the members of the Bureau and the chairs of national delegations. It meets at least twice yearly, and its main task is to act for the Assembly between plenary sessions. Every year, it meets in each of the two member states which are chairing the Committee of Ministers, for an exchange of views with the Chair.

Joint Committee

The Joint Committee comprises one representative of each member government, plus an equal number of Assembly representatives (members of the Bureau and one representative of each parliamentary delegation which is not represented on the Bureau). It acts as co-ordinating body between the Committee of Ministers and the Assembly, and is chaired by the latter's President.

Committees

The Assembly has 10 committees:

The Political Affairs Committee
The Committee on Legal Affairs and Human Rights
The Committee on Economic Affairs and Development
The Social, Health and Family Affairs Committee
The Committee on Migration, Refugees and Population
The Committee on Culture, Science and Education
The Committee on the Environment, Agriculture and Local and Regional Affairs
The Committee on Equal Opportunities for Women and Men
The Committee on Rules of Procedure and Immunities
The Committee on the Honouring of Obligations and Commitments by Member States of the Council of Europe (Monitoring Committee)

To further its work, a committee may establish one or more sub-committees, determining their terms of reference and membership on doing so.

3. How it operates

Sessions

The Assembly holds an annual ordinary session, which is divided into four week-long part-sessions. These take place in January, April, June and September-October in the Palais de l'Europe, Strasbourg.

Official languages

Under its Statute, the Council of Europe's official languages are English and French. German, Italian and Russian are Assembly working languages.

Adopted texts

The Assembly adopts three types of text: recommendations, resolutions and opinions.

- **Recommendations** contain proposals to the Committee of Ministers; implementing them is a matter for governments.

- **Resolutions** embody Assembly decisions on questions for which it is responsible, or express views which are its sole responsibility.

- **Opinions** are formulated by the Assembly on questions referred to it by the Committee of Ministers, for example the admission of new member states, and also on draft conventions and the budget.

Motions for recommendations or resolutions are usually the prelude to the preparation of a report. They must be tabled by 10 or more members belonging to at least five different national delegations. They are sent to one committee for report, and possibly others for opinion. The main committee appoints a rapporteur, who prepares a report in two parts: a draft resolution, recommendation or opinion, and an explanatory memorandum.

Both parts are examined in committee, but a vote is taken only on the first. Once adopted in committee, the report is tabled for debate by the Assembly, which examines it either at a part-session or at a meeting of the Standing Committee.

4. Communication

A web server gives members, national parliaments, governments and the public access to information and downloadable documents on the work of the Assembly. The Assembly's website – http://assembly.coe.int – gives access to:

– *News day by day:* press releases and communiqués;

– *PACE News:* electronic newsletter;

– *Parliamentary work:* meetings, sessions, conferences, agendas, working papers and adopted texts;

– *Composition of the Assembly:* President, members, committees, political groups and national delegations;

– *A document search engine*, site index, links to other Council of Europe websites, websites of national parliaments and international partners.

INDEX

The 46 parliamentary delegations to the Assembly and the number of representatives

Albania (4)
Andorra (2)
Armenia (4)
Austria (6)
Azerbaijan (6)
Belgium (7)
Bosnia and Herzegovina (5)
Bulgaria (6)
Cyprus (3)
Croatia (5)
Czech Republic (7)
Denmark (5)
Estonia (3)
Finland (5)
France (18)
Georgia (5)
Germany (18)
Greece (7)
Hungary (7)
Iceland (3)
Ireland (4)
Italy (18)
Latvia (3)
Liechtenstein (2)
Lithuania (4)
Luxembourg (3)
Malta (3)
Moldova (5)
Monaco (2)
Netherlands (7)
Norway (5)
Poland (12)
Portugal (7)
Romania (10)
Russian Federation (18)
San Marino (2)
Serbia (7)
Slovakia (5)
Slovenia (3)
Spain (12)
Sweden (6)
Switzerland (6)
The "former Yugoslav Republic of Macedonia" (3)
Turkey (12)
Ukraine (12)
United Kingdom (18)

Observer status

Israeli Knesset (1957)
Canadian Parliament (1997)
Mexican Parliament (1999)

The Assembly determines the size of observer delegations, which are not entitled to vote, but may speak when authorised to do so by the President.

Special Guest status

The Assembly introduced special guest status in 1989 to smooth the path to Council of Europe membership for the countries of central and eastern Europe. All the countries awarded this status have since joined – with the exception of Belarus, whose special guest status, granted on 16 September 1992, was suspended on 13 January 1997.

Sales agents for publications of the Council of Europe
Agents de vente des publications du Conseil de l'Europe

BELGIUM/BELGIQUE
La Librairie Européenne -
The European Bookshop
Rue de l'Orme, 1
B-1040 BRUXELLES
Tel.: +32 (0)2 231 04 35
Fax: +32 (0)2 735 08 60
E-mail: order@libeurop.be
http://www.libeurop.be

Jean De Lannoy
Avenue du Roi 202 Koningslaan
B-1190 BRUXELLES
Tel.: +32 (0)2 538 43 08
Fax: +32 (0)2 538 08 41
E-mail: jean.de.lannoy@dl-servi.com
http://www.jean-de-lannoy.be

**CANADA and UNITED STATES/
CANADA et ÉTATS-UNIS**
Renouf Publishing Co. Ltd.
1-5369 Canotek Road
OTTAWA, Ontario K1J 9J3, Canada
Tel.: +1 613 745 2665
Fax: +1 613 745 7660
Toll-Free Tel.: (866) 767-6766
E-mail: orders@renoufbooks.com
http://www.renoufbooks.com

**CZECH REPUBLIC/
RÉPUBLIQUE TCHÈQUE**
Suweco CZ, s.r.o.
Klecakova 347
CZ-180 21 PRAHA 9
Tel.: +420 2 424 59 204
Fax: +420 2 848 21 646
E-mail: import@suweco.cz
http://www.suweco.cz

DENMARK/DANEMARK
GAD
Vimmelskaftet 32
DK-1161 KØBENHAVN K
Tel.: +45 77 66 60 00
Fax: +45 77 66 60 01
E-mail: gad@gad.dk
http://www.gad.dk

FINLAND/FINLANDE
Akateeminen Kirjakauppa
PO Box 128
Keskuskatu 1
FIN-00100 HELSINKI
Tel.: +358 (0)9 121 4430
Fax: +358 (0)9 121 4242
E-mail: akatilaus@akateeminen.com
http://www.akateeminen.com

FRANCE
La Documentation française
(diffusion/distribution France entière)
124, rue Henri Barbusse
F-93308 AUBERVILLIERS CEDEX
Tél.: +33 (0)1 40 15 70 00
Fax: +33 (0)1 40 15 68 00
E-mail: prof@ladocumentationfrancaise.fr
http://www.ladocumentationfrancaise.fr

Librairie Kléber
1 rue des Francs Bourgeois
F-67000 STRASBOURG
Tel.: +33 (0)3 88 15 78 88
Fax: +33 (0)3 88 15 78 80
E-mail: francois.wolfermann@librairie-kleber.fr
http://www.librairie-kleber.com

**GERMANY/ALLEMAGNE
AUSTRIA/AUTRICHE**
UNO Verlag GmbH
August-Bebel-Allee 6
D-53175 BONN
Tel.: +49 (0)228 94 90 20
Fax: +49 (0)228 94 90 222
E-mail: bestellung@uno-verlag.de
http://www.uno-verlag.de

GREECE/GRÈCE
Librairie Kauffmann s.a.
Stadiou 28
GR-105 64 ATHINAI
Tel.: +30 210 32 55 321
Fax.: +30 210 32 30 320
E-mail: ord@otenet.gr
http://www.kauffmann.gr

HUNGARY/HONGRIE
Euro Info Service kft.
1137 Bp. Szent István krt. 12.
H-1137 BUDAPEST
Tel.: +36 (06)1 329 2170
Fax: +36 (06)1 349 2053
E-mail: euroinfo@euroinfo.hu
http://www.euroinfo.hu

ITALY/ITALIE
Licosa SpA
Via Duca di Calabria, 1/1
I-50125 FIRENZE
Tel.: +39 0556 483215
Fax: +39 0556 41257
E-mail: licosa@licosa.com
http://www.licosa.com

MEXICO/MEXIQUE
Mundi-Prensa México, S.A. De C.V.
Río Pánuco, 141 Delegacíon Cuauhtémoc
06500 MÉXICO, D.F.
Tel.: +52 (01)55 55 33 56 58
Fax: +52 (01)55 55 14 67 99
E-mail: mundiprensa@mundiprensa.com.mx
http://www.mundiprensa.com.mx

NETHERLANDS/PAYS-BAS
De Lindeboom Internationale Publicaties b.v.
M.A. de Ruyterstraat 20 A
NL-7482 BZ HAAKSBERGEN
Tel.: +31 (0)53 5740004
Fax: +31 (0)53 5729296
E-mail: books@delindeboom.com
http://www.delindeboom.com

NORWAY/NORVÈGE
Akademika
Postboks 84 Blindern
N-0314 OSLO
Tel.: +47 2 218 8100
Fax: +47 2 218 8103
E-mail: support@akademika.no
http://akademika.no

POLAND/POLOGNE
Ars Polona JSC
25 Obroncow Street
PL-03-933 WARSZAWA
Tel.: +48 (0)22 509 86 00
Fax: +48 (0)22 509 86 10
E-mail: arspolona@arspolona.com.pl
http://www.arspolona.com.pl

PORTUGAL
Livraria Portugal
(Dias & Andrade, Lda.)
Rua do Carmo, 70
P-1200-094 LISBOA
Tel.: +351 21 347 42 82 / 85
Fax: +351 21 347 02 64
E-mail: info@livrariaportugal.pt
http://www.livrariaportugal.pt

**RUSSIAN FEDERATION/
FÉDÉRATION DE RUSSIE**
Ves Mir
9a, Kolpacnhyi per.
RU-101000 MOSCOW
Tel.: +7 (8)495 623 6839
Fax: +7 (8)495 625 4269
E-mail: zimarin@vesmirbooks.ru
http://www.vesmirbooks.ru

SPAIN/ESPAGNE
Mundi-Prensa Libros, s.a.
Castelló, 37
E-28001 MADRID
Tel.: +34 914 36 37 00
Fax: +34 915 75 39 98
E-mail: liberia@mundiprensa.es
http://www.mundiprensa.com

SWITZERLAND/SUISSE
Van Diermen Editions – ADECO
Chemin du Lacuez 41
CH-1807 BLONAY
Tel.: +41 (0)21 943 26 73
Fax: +41 (0)21 943 36 05
E-mail: info@adeco.org
http://www.adeco.org

UNITED KINGDOM/ROYAUME-UNI
The Stationery Office Ltd
PO Box 29
GB-NORWICH NR3 1GN
Tel.: +44 (0)870 600 5522
Fax: +44 (0)870 600 5533
E-mail: book.enquiries@tso.co.uk
http://www.tsoshop.co.uk

**UNITED STATES and CANADA/
ÉTATS-UNIS et CANADA**
Manhattan Publishing Company
468 Albany Post Road
CROTTON-ON-HUDSON, NY 10520, USA
Tel.: +1 914 271 5194
Fax: +1 914 271 5856
E-mail: Info@manhattanpublishing.com
http://www.manhattanpublishing.com

Council of Europe Publishing/Editions du Conseil de l'Europe
F-67075 Strasbourg Cedex
Tel.: +33 (0)3 88 41 25 81 – Fax: +33 (0)3 88 41 39 10 – E-mail: publishing@coe.int – Website: http://book.coe.int